All Out of Faith

All Out of Faith

Southern Women on Spirituality

Edited by WENDY REED and JENNIFER HORNE

The University of Alabama Press
Tuscaloosa

Library of Congress Cataloging-in-Publication data will be found at the end of this book.

Permissions: "That Old-Time Religion" from *Womenfolks: Growing Up Down South,*
copyright © 1983 by Shirley Abbott, reprinted by permission of Houghton Mifflin and by
permission of the Wallace Literary Agency. All rights reserved. "This Is Our World," by
Dorothy Allison, from *Doubletake,* reprinted by permission of the author. "Why Jesus
Loved Whores," by Vicki Covington, from *Oxford American,* reprinted by permission of
the author. "Interview with Lee Smith" from *The Christ-Haunted Landscape: Faith and
Doubt in Southern Fiction* by Susan Ketchin, University Press of Mississippi, 1994, re-
printed by permission of Susan Ketchin and University Press of Mississippi. "Awakening"
from *The Dance of the Dissident Daughter* by Sue Monk Kidd, copyright © 1996 by Sue
Monk Kidd, reprinted by permission of HarperCollins Publishers. "The Making of a
Preacher's Wife," by Cassandra King, used by permission of the author. "Knowing Our
Place," by Barbara Kingsolver, from *Small Wonder: Essays by Barbara Kingsolver,* copy-
right © 2002 by Barbara Kingsolver, reprinted by permission of HarperCollins Publishers.
"Relics of Summer" from *Under the Tuscan Sun* by Francis Mayes, copyright © Frances
Mayes, used by permission of Chronicle Books LLC, San Francisco. "From Birmingham
to Redemption," by Diane McWhorter, used by permission of the author. "Full Circle"
from *Pauli Murray: The Autobiography of a Black Activist, Feminist, Lawyer, Priest, and
Poet* by Pauli Murray, courtesy of Charlotte Sheedy Literary Agency, New York. "When
Woods Are Dark: The Enchantment of the Infinite," by Sena Jeter Naslund, used by permission of the author. "Sex, Race, and the Stained-Glass Window" from *Women and
Therapy* 19:4 (December 31, 1996) by Nzinga Shaka Zulu (Sylvia Rhue), reprinted by permission of Haworth Press, Binghamton, N.Y. "Becoming a Cantor," by Jessica Roskin,
used by permission of the author. "I Lead Two Lives: Confessions of a Closet Baptist,"
by Mab Segrest, from *Speaking for Ourselves: Women of the South,* edited by Maxine
Alexander, reprinted by permission of the author. "Where the Spirit Moved Me," by
Jeanie Thompson, used by permission of the author. "A Baptist-Buddhist," by Jan Willis,
from *Dreaming Me: An African American Woman's Spiritual Journey,* by Jan Willis, reprinted by permission of the author.

For my sisters, Jan and Brenda, and my children, Brittany, Brianne, and Reed

WENDY REED

For my mother, Dodie Walton Horne, and my sister, Mary Thach Horne

JENNIFER HORNE

Contents

Acknowledgments

The editors would like to thank the women in their families, for sharing a legacy of love and laughter, and the women in this collection, whose courage and inspiration made it possible in the first place. They also wish to thank the following: Debbie Bammerlin, Candy Cooper, Judy Derieux, Amy Eifler, Greg Hagler, Tammy Holloway, Angela O'Connor, and Kathryn Valencia for their gift of friendship; Nancy Campbell, Sharon Devaney-Lovinguth, Rachel Dobson, Jennifer Fremlin, Jane Green, Mary Horne, Gretchen McCullough, and Susan Rogers for their helpful and insightful conversations about Southern women, spirituality, and the formation of this book; Wayne Flynt, Greg Garrison, and Stan Ingersol, whose work in the area of Southern religion continues to influence; Frances Mason, Henry Joiner, Larry Wimberly, Buddy Gray, Sarah Jackson Shelton, June Bruce, and Nell Turner Pugh for sharing their faith by example; Patrick Green, for sharing his knowledge of religious studies; the staff of the University of Alabama Center for Public Television and Radio for encouraging creativity and tolerance across a variety of media; the staff of the Sanford Media Resource and Design Center at the University of Alabama's Gorgas Library for their invaluable technological assistance; and, finally, Jon Berry, Jo Few, Dick and Nancy Horne, Don Noble, and Betty Reed for support and encouragement along the way.

Introduction

We do not burn the bodies of women today; but we humiliate them in a thousand ways, and chiefly by our theologies.
—Elizabeth Cady Stanton

There was the method of kneeling,
a fine method,
if you lived in a country
where stones were smooth.
Naomi Shihab Nye, from "Different Ways to Pray"

Call it what you will—theology, an opiate, an oppressor, a right, the right, or the right and only way—religion and its interpretations continue, as always, to stimulate. To excite. To discriminate. Especially in the South, where the largest religious group, the 16 million-member Southern Baptist Convention, is the spiritual equivalent of a Microsoft operating system.

While not every Southerner is religious, every Southerner has been shaped by religion in some form or fashion. (Some might call it warped rather than shaped.) In this collection, narrative allows us to glimpse the shaping. Somehow, any story or narrative or discussion of religion comes back to the notion of an operating system and how we navigate through it, or around it, as some have managed to do. Too often, operating systems tend toward hierarchies, and hierarchies suggest control. Someone is told what to do here, what not to do there. Still, Flannery O'Connor managed to find grace.

Some say the Southern landscape does not hinder such findings at all but helps writers as they search for truth through the word.

The Word is, after all, believed by some to be the real beginning. But which Word, and then which translation?

The title is no accident. Religion has drained the life out of some of the most faithful people we know. And yet that it has lifted others to heights can only be explained as miraculous. This collection is not intended as a prescription. It should not be read for absolutes. Rather, we hope these stories, presented together, sound out some unspoken truths, so that those who may not understand belief in easy terms may understand they are not alone.

Our goal has been to present as wide and varied a view as possible of Southern women's responses to and reflections on spirituality and organized religion. In a region first identified in the 1920s by H. L. Mencken as the "Bible Belt," religion is still a pervasive presence, whether in debates over the Ten Commandments in the courtroom, women in the pulpit, public prayer at the weekly high school football game, or Sunday liquor sales. We want to explore how women see themselves fitting into—or not—such a religious culture, and where they locate their spirituality. Is women's spirituality different from men's? Some of these essays suggest it is. We are wary, however, of creating a "separate but equal" category for women, given the ways in which the world's major religions have historically oppressed women by suggesting that they have a special role to play, one that does not involve leadership.

We consider religion as having to do with regular religious practice, with a defined set of beliefs and a particular tradition, whereas spirituality refers more to one's sense of connection to the divine or the sacred, and connection to others, and to the search for meaning in one's life. Spirituality may be expressed in a religious setting; religion does not necessarily produce spirituality.

As a measure of the importance of Christianity in the South, *The Statistical Abstract of the United States* (2001) indicates that the percentage of those in Southern states who identify themselves as Christian regularly falls between 60 and 70 percent, as compared with, for instance, 39 percent in New Hampshire, 39 percent in California, and 32 percent in Oregon. Only the Midwest comes close to the South, and many consider it to be an extension of the Bible Belt.

In *The Encyclopedia of Southern Culture* (1989), Thomas R. Frazier writes that, due to "the patriarchal emphasis of the culture," women have rarely been involved in the founding of new religious movements. Rather, he writes, "Southern women have channeled their spiritual energies into the traditional religious structure. Those who have been unable to fit into the cultural mold have either left the region or turned inward upon themselves and nurtured their spiritual lives. The stifling of southern women's spiritual insights has led some of these women to seek self-fulfillment in areas outside the life of the churches, an enterprise that only today is meeting with any degree of success." With this book, we wish to give voice to those who have found a way to stay, those who have stayed but are struggling, and those who have left but still maintain some kind of spiritual life.

Spiritual struggles, awakenings, transformations, and rebellions don't fit easily into categories. The three suggested above—those who've stayed, those who've struggled, and those who've left— suggest a possible rubric for discussing the essays chosen for this book. But other similarities arise as well: Frances Mayes and Barbara Kingsolver both write about the importance of nature and of place, Mayes going all the way to Italy to remember her Georgia religious upbringing and Kingsolver writing of the two significant places in her life, desert Arizona and the Southern Appalachians. Dorothy Allison, Cassandra King, and Jeanie Thompson write of the transformative power of art. The first work of art Allison loved was a painting of Jesus, while King, struggling with the rigid role requirements of being a preacher's wife, found herself through writing. Thompson talks of the place she enters through poetry, which she describes as "fundamentally a transcendental act." Shirley

Abbott, Sena Jeter Naslund, and Lee Smith all went through powerful early experiences with religious fervor—each reflects on what role those brushes with the mystical and mysterious had on their lives. As a child, Shirley Abbott was bound and determined to be saved and was willing to endure a rigorous routine at a remote church camp in pursuit of salvation; Sena Jeter Naslund recalls how an early experience with fundamentalist doctrines of faith taught her to accept herself as she was; Lee Smith recalls the excitement of being saved, not once but many times, until her parents made her stop. Of these fifteen pieces, Pauli Murray, the first black female Episcopal priest, and Jessica Roskin, who became a Jewish cantor, are the only two to remain fully within their original religious tradition while expanding the boundaries of that tradition. Jan Willis defines herself as a "Baptist-Buddhist," a longtime practicing Buddhist who nevertheless does not reject her early Baptist upbringing. Vicki Covington, Mab Segrest, and Sue Monk Kidd chronicle life crises related to their faith—Covington of the complex relationship between sexuality and religion; Segrest of being a closeted lesbian teacher in a Baptist school; Kidd of an awakening to a feminist spirituality that shook her life to its roots. Sylvia Rhue describes the racism, sexism, and homophobia that caused her to leave the church—then argues for a compassionate understanding of those still suffering from those "ism's" and phobias.

We know the *New Testament* claims that Jesus had sisters, but we don't know their names. Because personal journeys don't always fit neatly into the lessons of organized religion, we wanted to celebrate the identities of those who have written about such journeys. Our own list of names, the women who speak up and speak out in this book, follows: Shirley Abbott, Dorothy Allison, Vicki Covington, Sue Monk Kidd, Cassandra King, Barbara Kingsolver, Frances Mayes, Diane McWhorter, Pauli Murray, Sena Jeter Naslund, Sylvia Rhue, Jessica Roskin, Mab Segrest, Lee Smith, Jeanie Thompson, and Jan Willis.

It is our hope that these women's voices, as varied and vulnerable and searching as any prophets' have ever been, will echo beyond traditional lines and reach women like, and not like, us. The women whose stories are gathered here have things to say about religion, about personal faith and belief, about disillusionment and reconnection, ceremonies both communal and individual.

Sacrifice isn't new to religion. Most celebrate it in some way with rituals of shedding the old self and being born again with a new self. These women have sacrificed by sharing their stories, by offering themselves up to us, being honest in ways that some might judge or look down on. Their words are part sacrifice, part communion. They commune with us by offering their stories. For their courage and openness, we thank them.

That Old-Time Religion

SHIRLEY ABBOTT

Anybody who grows up in the South may have to reckon, some time or another, with being born again. When I was a child, the religious fervor of my mother's family had faded to a phantom of its old self. They did not testify about the love of Jesus or shout in unknown tongues on Sunday mornings or even read the Bible at night and say grace at table. Yet they had not quite shaken off all ties with the hard-shell faith of the backwoods.

Most people I knew went to church, even if they omitted standing up and hollering. Occasionally they would go to a revival meeting and allow themselves to be shaken by it. And if you asked them, they'd tell you it was a sin to dance and smoke and drink, even though they did all these things once in a while. They still believed in heaven and hell and in the stark truths of the Bible, though they had quit reading it. Least of all had any of them questioned the foundation of all fundamentalist doctrine: that getting to heaven was a matter of one lone, orgasmic confrontation between the soul and Jesus. After that, even if the fleshly self insisted on visiting honky-tonks or breaking half the Ten Commandments, the soul within would one day return to righteousness, for it could never be lost.

My father, transplanted Yankee that he was, held the Baptists and their ilk in contempt. With his selective affinity for Southern culture, he slung the Baptists into some nether category of ignoramuses, along with people who put cow-dung poultices on broken bones and believed in hoop snakes. His inclination, when it came to my religious training, was to school me in Methodism. He didn't mean some walleyed, floor-stomping Methodism that had moved to town from the mountains. He meant something entirely unSouthern, with no taint of emotionalism. Something urban. A church that christened babies and sprinkled the forelocks of new members and had a minister with a tangle of DDs and LLs after his name who quoted Sir Walter Scott and Wordsworth and Browning and in any case, at the end of the sermon, did not launch into an unseemly tantrum about walking on down the aisle to get saved.

But my father's desire to turn me into a respectable Christian was much too slight to energize him, let alone me. How could he expect me to take Sunday school seriously when most often on Sunday afternoons, after we had gorged ourselves on fried chicken and cream gravy, Daddy read aloud to me from Gibbon? On the Lord's day he was almost deliberate about picking passages on the early Christians and how they had made a nuisance of themselves to the Romans. Edward Gibbon perceives the saintly band as a burden borne with commendable patience by the Roman upper classes, much as in his day the upper crust had to put up with Wesleyans and Luddites. This was the one time my father chose not to take the side of the underdog. He did not construe Christians as underdogs. They were, he knew very well, constantly trying to deprive him of his livelihood. To the Hot Springs Protestant Church Council, open gambling was the work of the anti-Christ, and they would have liked to see all bookies in jail. Daddy could deposit me all brushed and ruffled on the front steps of the First Methodist church as many Sundays as he cared to, but I never forgot which side he was on when it came to lions versus Christians.

Still, I was too young to join him in agnosticism, and when I slipped out of the Methodist net (my absence unfeelingly ignored by them), I fell heavily into the Baptist one. This was not because my mother had pushed me toward her ancestral faith, but because the Baptists in a small Southern town make it their business to pick up stragglers. My mother, at least while I lived under her roof, never went to church regularly. Yet she had come out of the raw old tradition. I had snapshots of her on baptizing day—forty youngsters in white sheets, up to their waists in the North Fork River and scared to death, about to be dunked by a preacher who looked seven feet tall and had hands the size of shovels. When I was a child, however, something about religion embarrassed her. Most other mothers I knew went dutifully from Sunday school to prayer meeting to Circle (where they talked about foreign missions) to choir practice to Sunday vespers, and they hauled their daughters along with them. I suspect that the women went for one another's company more than Jesus' sake, but in any case, they went.

And I began to go, too, about the time I turned thirteen—the classic moment for the fundamentalist God to bring in the sheaves. Of course, my attraction to religion had something sexual in it. The preacher at the Baptist church, ambivalently named Vergil Luther Radley, was a massive, good-looking man of about thirty-five, swarthy, brown-eyed, broad-faced, thin-mouthed, and powerfully muscled. The effect was Laurence Olivier as Othello. Brother Radley's suits were white, his Bible black. (Surely he switched to black broadcloth in the winter, but I recall only the white.) Even if he had not been young and handsome, he was a man. Not just a man, but an actor, a dancer, a performer. To young virgins such as

I, he projected an almost lurid masculinity, which I loved—not knowing why or what—but knew I oughtn't to be sensing. Most Baptist ministers kept their masculinity tucked so far back that one would have sworn they were neuters. Not Brother Radley—he flaunted it, at least from the safety of the pulpit. And under his pastorate, the church flourished.

Working with the intelligence of a premier danseur or a quarterback running a complicated play, he could in three-quarters of an hour work himself up to the classic Baptist frenzy. To the unpracticed eye, it might look uncontrolled, but one quickly learned what to expect. I relished the performance. First, with exaggerated calm, he read the Scriptures and prayed—maybe it was Saul on the road to Damascus. Before long he'd be crouching behind the lectern, the fiery black eyes staring just over the top of it as he gripped the front edge in his right hand. "Saul, Saul," he would cry out, as though the heavens had parted, "Why persecutest thou Me?" Then he'd thrust his long fingers into his breast pocket, rip out a white handkerchief, flourish it, tamp his agonized forehead with it, and wad it up, while at the end of his other arm the Bible flapped as if he meant to lob it into the top balcony. The baritone voice, rich as chocolate, sometimes bubbled with a sob. All this gesture he enhanced by darting to and fro, leaping up, slapping the Book. And as if a gale were blowing across the altar, the thick swatch of his coal-dark hair swept across his countenance and fell into his eyes.

Finally stepping out from behind the lectern, planting his feet on the high ground and showing himself full length to the congregation, he would raise his hands skyward and cry out, "Don't remain in the darkness of sin denying Jesus. Come, come to your savior. Get up and come on down to Him and be saved." Then Brother Radley would open his arms to receive us, while the piano began to strum, and the choir murmured, "Just as I am, O Lamb of God,

I come," or "There is a fountain filled with blood, drawn from Immanuel's veins." Many would be weeping aloud, and I always trembled in my pew. I had no idea what feelings—apart from the spiritual—he was playing upon in me, and neither, I believe, did he. It was all part of the preaching art, and he was good at it. I am certain that he was a rigorously faithful husband with never a roving thought.

On Sunday morning, weak-kneed and sobbing, I did go down that aisle for him. Yes, and he folded me in those white-clad arms, briefly pressed my cheek against his heaving chest, cupped my chin in his hand, and looked into my eyes. At his gentle command, I bowed my head and listened to him pray for me, thank God for me, thank Jesus that this fine young girl had come to accept Him as her Savior and Lord.

The trouble was that I was faking. Oh, I signed the card. I asked to be immersed. I sat down on the front pew and prayed with all my strength, waiting for the proper psychic jolt. Hanging on. Tensing my muscles. Even, I recall, uttering a groan or two. But it didn't happen. Apart from my now subsiding stage fright, I didn't feel any different than I had before. Soon after my baptism in the comfortably warm font, I was elected president of my Sunday school class. Lent my enthusiastic voice to the choir. Resolved to remain a nonsmoker and a pure teetotaler. Was outspoken in my disapproval of dancing—another adult skill I hadn't quite acquired. But even as I stood in the baptismal tank with a white sheet over my swimsuit, even as Brother Radley put one hand behind my shoulders, squeezed my nose shut with the other, and laid me back in the water, I knew I was a fraud.

I didn't give up hope. Maybe I could get right with God. All it took, they said, was "conviction of sin"; that is, I had to believe I deserved to go to hell, and I did believe it. And then I had to believe

Jesus could save me. And I believed that, too. But for all that, it was like memorizing the rules of golf and then, out on the green, discovering that it couldn't be done.

My profoundest struggle to be born again came a couple of years later when I decided, to my father's disgust, to spend two weeks at the Baptist church camp at Siloam Springs, in the northwestern, almost primeval, corner of Arkansas. Over the two-lane roads of the day, it was at least a five-hour drive from home. Twelve or thirteen girls and three or four boys were going to church camp, the lot of us meticulously chaperoned by a pair of young marrieds who had temporarily foresworn the privileges of matrimony in order to shepherd us to Siloam. We set off from the church parking lot early one June morning in an ancient gray Sunday school bus with "Second Baptist" in big black letters on the side. The seats had no springs, and the hot wind cut scathingly through the open windows. We sang all the way—hymnbooks had been provided— which kept us occupied and drowned out the ominous knocks in the engine and the horrid screechings of the transmission when, on the slightest upgrade, the driver had to downshift.

Siloam, in the New Testament, is the spring outside Jerusalem where Jesus works a miracle: he sends a blind man there to wash his eyes and recover his sight. My eyes, as I approached Siloam, were blind in some sense, too. The camp site was a leafy mountain glade traversed by a brook. In the center, green and well tended, was a kind of campus with a large tent pitched over a wooden amphitheater built on the slope of a hill. On the other side of this lawn was a whitewashed dining hall. The dormitories teetered at a distance on the surrounding hills, on stilts. Boys were well separated from the girls. Instead of toilets, there were latrines, and water gushed (sometimes) from the end of a handpump. Swimming was not allowed since one needed a bathing suit to swim, and flesh was ipso facto immoral. Shorts and slacks were also forbidden, at least for the girls. Even sundresses were classed as not nice. We slept in cots in the screened-in dormitories and had no semblance of privacy—no possibility of reading or writing letters in bed. No books. No telephones. Not even some small crossroads Jerusalem to walk to and spend a quarter at the country store. Siloam was all there was.

At six we arose, dressed beside our cots, washed our faces at the pump, and heard an hour of preaching before breakfast. Afterward there were Bible classes, followed by more preaching. Lunch was at noon, and then we had a free hour before crafts classes. We made earbobs out of shells. Supper began at five. The dining room was far too small, and we languished, starving, in long lines, relieving the tedium with a lot of nervous adolescent flirting and raucous choruses of hymns. The meals consisted of canned vegetables, along with fried potatoes, hot dogs (limp), hamburgers (fried thin and crisp), huge stacks of white bread, and gluey fruit pies. Fortunately food was irrelevant to most of us.

Preaching began again just after supper and usually lasted until ten. This was the real service. At morning and noon the preachers and song leaders were most often students from some local Bible college, but at night we had the full professional complement, including what must have been the highest-stepping, loudest revival preacher in Arkansas. He frightened me. Brother Radley was always terrifying enough, with his hoarse invocations of hellfire and his implicit contempt for most human activities conducted outside sanctuary walls. But at least he was a DD, and he had those dark eyes. This red-faced evangelist made Radley look like an Episcopalian rector. In my inmost heart, he aroused no feeling of tenderness.

He shouted, strutted, and stamped, described all the torments of hell, including pincers and demons jamming the red-hot picks right into you, under your fingernails. He claimed that right here in this fine camp half the young people who thought they were saved weren't. If we were really saved, we'd be down here on our hands and knees at the altar, dedicating our lives to Christian service. We'd be pledging ourselves to become music directors, especially all us talented girls, or looking to marry ministers and be good helpmeets to them, or we'd be thinking about foreign missions. We'd be searching our souls for a vocation and praying to God. Instead, what were we doing? Unmindful of our immortal souls, according to him, we were strolling off into the darkness together in mixed couples, sitting down, boy next to girl, on benches at nightfall, not even bothering to come into the tent for the service. It turned his stomach to have to say it. (I had myself somewhat wistfully observed a pair of bench sitters: a crew-cut youth holding the hand of a girl whose blond perfection clearly paralyzed him. But they said he was a future preacher, and she was his betrothed.) Everybody else squirmed when he said this, as though guilty of multiple fornication. The counsellors looked stricken. I was relieved. This was the only charge of his that failed to nail me to the wall.

As the days went on, and the preaching got hotter, my soul festered. I was overwhelmed by my unholy state. I pleaded with the Lord to flood my soul with the right feelings. How could anybody want so desperately to be born again and not be able to slip through? The preacher said nobody had ever been turned away. But in addition to all this angst, I loathed standing in lines for meals. I yearned for a real bath. It stayed mercilessly hot, and it never rained. The mosquitoes finally died of the drought. I missed my mother, my books, my own bed. And in the middle of my deepest prayers my eyes would fill with pictures of strolling couples, and I would yearn to be led off into the twilight by one of those bad, backsliding boys.

Alas, there were no brief encounters. Life in the gulag went on—but only for its term. On the last evening, supper turned out to be ham, green beans, and potato salad—truly a banquet after what had gone before. I ate big helpings of everything, in spite of a faint metallic edge in the meat. I wondered why the milk was warm, and drank water instead. Then I went cheerfully off to the meeting. I knew they had cranked up for a coda, and if Jesus didn't claim me tonight, He never would. Tonight I meant to get religion, or else I'd bow out.

We sang more hymns than usual, and the preachers, as expected, painted hell as hotter than usual. When at last we stood for the invitation, I discovered I was so giddy I had to hang on to the back of the folding chair in front of me. "Amazing grace, how sweet the sound, that saved a wretch like me. I once was lost but now am found, was blind but now I see." Blind but now I see. The words scorched me, seared me, as though I had not previously understood the English language and now miraculously did. I felt faint, but someone caught my arm, and I didn't fall. Instead, my transfiguration began. The tears ran, the light under the tent turned a vivid yellow, and sobbing loudly, I battled my way down the rows and joined the throng that by now was pressing toward the altar. This was it. I had done it. We had done it. I felt a surge of joy that could only be the certifiable, genuine thing. I quaked and sweated. When at last some toiler in the vineyards finally led me to a chair, I signed two cards, one professing my faith in the Lord and testifying to my salvation and another stating my intention to become a missionary in Africa.

That night I twitched upon my cot—one cannot thrash on a couch so hard and narrow—trying to control my sense of elated dislocation, wishing I could sleep but disturbed by technicolor dreams whenever I did drop off. At dawn I got up and read the Bible—as the preacher had admonished us newborns to do. I drank the pump water with a drunkard's thirst and settled down to Revelations. But the words uncoupled themselves from one another on the page, and I could extract no meaning from them.

Bewildered and exhausted, I dressed and packed, then went down to wait for breakfast. Today the morning service was omitted. Bus time was eight. I had to sit down on the ground while waiting in line, and then found I could not eat. Was this rebirth? I wept waiting for the gray bus to roll up. I thought about the Africans. I figured they'd be standing in a line waiting for me, and what would I tell them? I'd be real nice. I'd hold the babies and not make a fuss if the women didn't wear blouses. Everybody would love me. Where would the mission board send me? The Congo? Nigeria? I'd go wherever they said.

The bus ride down from Siloam was as jolting and hot as the trip up, but this time nobody felt like singing. I stretched out on the long padded bench in the back of the bus and slept. I woke, occasionally, and remembered what my father had told me one time about certain tropical parasites that build their homes in people's muscles, just below the skin. I thought about leeches and tsetse flies. Kraits. Bugs that burrowed into your eyeballs and made you blind. Was blind but now I see. They liked us to come back from camp rejoicing, so our counsellors woke us up in time for a weak chorus of "That Old Time Religion" as we rounded the corner and stopped in front of the church. Brother Radley, his dark face set into a smile, was waiting to receive us. I descended from the bus, shook his hand, and wobbled into the arms of my father and mother.

I had food poisoning, of course. It set in explosively just as my anxious mother led me inside the back door. The retching was over in a few hours, but the fever lasted several days. I couldn't remember ever being so sick. I slept as if drugged for forty-eight hours. When I revived and recalled that I was now among the elect, I began to read brief passages of Charles Sheldon's *In His Steps,* which somebody gave me the night of the cataclysm. The notion of the book, which I later learned is one of the all-time best sellers, is that before doing or saying anything, one must ask oneself whether Jesus would have done or said it, and how.

Would Jesus have drunk the glass of ginger ale my mother had just given me? Was there a Baptist position on soda pop? Mother was reading aloud from the *Arkansas Gazette*. An item on an inside page reported an epidemic of food poisoning among teenagers around the state, which had been traced to a failure of refrigeration at Siloam Springs Baptist Church Camp. Perhaps half the five hundred campers and staff had been affected, but no deaths had been reported. "So," I thought, lapsing quickly into my rationalist mode, "the buggers let the food go bad and then fed it to us anyhow." Christlike once more, I forgave them. As my strength came back, I ceased asking Jesus about every breath I took. My heart unburdened itself of unsaved souls in the Congo and Nigeria. My hard-won piety was all gone, along with the salmonella. I continued to go to church a few years more, but if I had been reborn at Siloam, it wasn't as a Baptist.

What I did not realize was that I had had a dangerous brush with history. Years later, in search of something else, I came across a report of an 1830s camp meeting. A great revival was sweeping the American frontier in those days, from Indiana to Kentucky to Tennessee. The reporter was Frances Trollope, the English traveller whose *Domestic Manners of the Americans,* published in 1832, was a fair account of what ruffians a brand-new people can be. The food was better, and the preaching wilder in her day, but Mrs. Trollope could just as well have been reporting from Siloam Springs.

"It was in the course of this summer," she wrote, "that I found the opportunity I had long wished for, of attending a camp meeting . . . in a wild district on the confines of Indiana. The prospect

of passing a night in the backwoods . . . was by no means agree-
able, but I screwed my courage to the proper pitch."

When she reached the spot "on the verge of an unbroken forest," she found tents of various sizes pitched in a circle, including
one for blacks. (Siloam was lily white of course, but the early frontier Baptists and Methodists welcomed everybody.) From every
tent came the sounds of "praying, preaching, singing and lamen-
tation." What caught her eye at once was a handsome youth of
about eighteen with his arms round a disheveled-looking girl, "her
features working with the most violent agitation." A "tall, trim
figure in black" was praying and preaching, and the young man
and woman soon fell forward, twitching on the straw floor of the
tent. In every tent was the same scene:

All were strewn with straw, and the distorted figures that we saw kneeling,
sitting and lying among it, joined to the woeful and compulsive cries, gave
to each the air of a cell in Bedlam.

Above a hundred persons, nearly all females, came forward, uttering
howlings and groans so terrible that I shall never cease to shudder when I
recall them. They appeared to draw each other forward, and on the word
being given, "let us pray," they all fell forward on their knees, but this posture was soon changed for others that permitted greater scope for the con-
vulsive movements of their limbs; and they were soon all lying on the
ground in an indescribable confusion of heads and legs . . . I felt sick with
horror.

Many of these wretched creatures were beautiful young females. The
preachers moved among them at once exciting and soothing their agonies.
I saw the insidious lips approach the cheeks of the unhappy girls; I heard
the murmured confessions of the poor victims, and I watched their tor-
mentors, breathing into their ears consolations that tinged the pale cheek
with red.

The praying and shouting went on all night. One woman shouted, over and over, "I will hold fast to Jesus, I never will let him go; if they take me to hell, I will still hold him fast, fast, fast.

But then to Mrs. Trollope's admitted astonishment, after a brief rest at dawn, "I saw the whole camp as joyously and eagerly employed in preparing and devouring their most substantial breakfasts as if the night had been passed in dancing; and I marked many a fair but pale face, that I recognized as a demoniac of the night, simpering beside a swain, to whom she carefully administered hot coffee and eggs. The preaching saint and the howling sinners seemed alike to relish this mode of recruiting their strength."

Ending her account, Mrs. Trollope makes a tart remark about the large amounts of money hauled in by the preachers, to be spent, presumably, on Bibles, tracts, and, she snorts, "all other religious purposes." Her sympathy with the camp meeting mentality was slight. Yet she caught all the essentials. Not merely the hysteria of the women and the shouts of the preachers, but the sexuality of it of which she vigorously disapproved. She dimly sensed the sociability; it gave the eighteen-year-olds a chance to do some serious courting. She seemed not to grasp that on the frontier this was the one true form of recreation available. It terrified her to see the people jump and shout, let alone roll around on the green earth. Then to her astonishment, what had appeared to be mass psychosis vanished with the rising sun. Saints and sinners had a decent breakfast, and Mrs. Trollope went elsewhere. So, no doubt, did everybody else, for they all had other business to look after. One cannot shout and tremble indefinitely—every party comes to an end. So, having completed a ritual that was to serve the purposes of country folk for at least another century—and in particular, I believe, the purposes of women—they hitched their teams to the wagons and drove home.

This Is Our World

DOROTHY ALLISON

The first painting I ever saw up close was at a Baptist church when I was seven years old. It was a few weeks before my mama was to be baptized. From it, I took the notion that art should surprise and astonish, and hopefully make you think something you had not thought until you saw it. The painting was a mural of Jesus at the Jordan River done on the wall behind the baptismal font. The font itself was a remarkable creation—a swimming pool with one glass side set into the wall above and behind the pulpit so that ordinarily you could not tell the font was there, seeing only the painting of Jesus. When the tank was flooded with water, little lights along the bottom came on, and anyone who stepped down the steps seemed to be walking past Jesus himself and descending into the Jordan River. Watching baptisms in that tank was like watching movies at the drive-in, my cousins had told me. From the moment the deacon walked us around the church, I knew what my cousin had meant. I could not take my eyes off the painting or the glass-fronted tank. It looked every moment as if Jesus were about to come alive, as if he were about to step out onto the water of the river. I think the way I stared at the painting made the deacon nervous.

The deacon boasted to my mama that there was nothing like that baptismal font in the whole state of South Carolina. It had been designed, he told her, by a nephew of the minister—a boy who had gone on to build a shopping center out in New Mexico. My mama was not sure that someone who built shopping centers was the kind of person who should have been designing baptismal fonts, and she was even more uncertain about the steep steps by Jesus' left hip. She asked the man to let her practice going up and down, but he warned her it would be different once the water poured in.

"It's quite safe though," he told her. "The water will hold you up. You won't fall."

I kept my attention on the painting of Jesus. He was much larger than I was, a little bit more than life-size, but the thick layer of shellac applied to protect the image acted like a magnifying glass, making him seem larger still. It was Jesus himself that fascinated me, though. He was all rouged and pale and pouty as Elvis Presley. This was not my idea of the Son of God, but I liked it. I liked it a lot.

"Jesus looks like a girl," I told my mama.

She looked up at the painted face. A little blush appeared on her cheekbones, and she looked as if she would have smiled if the deacon were not frowning so determinedly. "It's just the eyelashes," she said. The deacon nodded. They climbed back up the stairs. I stepped over close to Jesus and put my hand on the painted robe. The painting was sweaty and cool, slightly oily under my fingers.

"I liked that Jesus," I told my mama as we walked out of the church. "I wish we had something like that." To her credit, Mama did not laugh.

"If you want a picture of Jesus," she said, "we'll get you one. They have them in nice frames at Sears." I sighed. That was not what I had in mind. What I wanted was a life-size, sweaty painting, one in which Jesus looked as hopeful as a young girl—something otherworldly and peculiar, but kind of wonderful at the same time. After that, every time we went to church I asked to go up to see the painting, but the baptismal font was locked tight when not in use.

The Sunday Mama was to be baptized, I watched the minister step down into that pool past the Son of God. The preacher's gown was tailored with little weights carefully sewn into the hem to keep it from rising up in the water. The water pushed up at the fabric while the weights tugged it down. Once the minister was all the way down into the tank, the robe floated up a bit so that it seemed to have a shirred ruffle all along the bottom. That was almost enough to pull my eyes away from the face of Jesus, but not quite. With the lights on in the bottom of the tank, the eyes of the painting seemed to move and shine. I tried to point it out to my sisters, but they were uninterested. All they wanted to see was Mama.

Mama was to be baptized last, after three little boys, and their gowns had not had any weights attached. The white robes floated up around their necks so that their skinny boy bodies and white cotton underwear were perfectly visible to the congregation. The water that came up above the hips of the minister lapped their shoulders, and the shortest of the boys seemed panicky at the prospect of gulping water, no matter how holy. He paddled furiously to keep above the water's surface. The water started to rock violently at his struggles, sweeping the other boys off their feet. All of them pumped their knees to stay upright and the minister, realizing how the scene must appear to the congregation below, speeded up the baptismal process, praying over and dunking the boys at high speed.

Around me the congregation shifted in their seats. My little sister slid forward off the pew, and I quickly grabbed her around the waist and barely stopped myself from laughing out loud. A titter from the back of the church indicated that other people were having the same difficulty keeping from laughing. Other people shifted irritably and glared at the noisemakers. It was clear that no matter the provocation, we were to pretend nothing funny was happening. The minister frowned more fiercely and prayed louder. My mama's friend Louise, sitting at our left, whispered a soft "Look at that" and we all looked up in awe. One of the hastily blessed boys had dog-paddled over to the glass and was staring out at us, eyes wide and his hands pressed flat to the glass. He looked as if he hoped someone would rescue him. It was too much for me. I began to giggle helplessly, and not a few of the people around me joined in. Impatiently the minister hooked the boy's robe, pulled him back, and pushed him toward the stairs.

My mama, just visible on the staircase, hesitated briefly as the sodden boy climbed up past her. Then she set her lips tightly together, and reached down and pressed her robe to her thighs. She came down the steps slowly, holding down the skirt as she did so, giving one stern glance to the two boys climbing past her up the steps, and then turning her face deliberately up to the painting of Jesus. Every move she made communicated resolution and faith, and the congregation stilled in respect. She was baptized looking up stubbornly, both hands holding down that cotton robe while below I fought so hard not to giggle, tears spilled down my face.

Over the pool, the face of Jesus watched solemnly with his pink, painted cheeks and thick, dark lashes. For all the absurdity of the event, his face seemed to me startlingly compassionate and wise. That face understood fidgety boys and stubborn women. It made me want the painting even more, and to this day I remember it with longing. It had the weight of art, that face. It had what I am sure art is supposed to have—the power to provoke, the authority of a heartfelt vision.

I imagine the artist who painted the baptismal font in that Baptist church so long ago was a man who did not think himself much of an artist. I have seen paintings like his many times since, so perhaps he worked from a model. Maybe he traced that face off another he had seen in some other church. For a while, I tried to imagine him a character out of a Flannery O'Connor short story, a man who traveled around the South in the fifties painting Jesus wherever he was needed, giving the Son of God the long lashes and pink cheeks of a young girl. He would be the kind of man who would see nothing blasphemous in painting eyes that followed the congregation as they moved up to the pulpit to receive a blessing and back to the pews to sit chastened and still for the benediction. Perhaps he had no sense of humor, or perhaps he had one too refined for intimidation. In my version of the story, he would have a case of whiskey in his van, right behind the gallon containers of shellac and buried notebooks of his own sketches. Sometimes, he would read thick journals of art criticism while sitting up late in cheap hotel rooms and then get roaring drunk and curse his fate.

"What I do is wallpaper," he would complain. "Just wallpaper." But the work he so despised would grow more and more famous as time passed. After his death, one of those journals would publish a careful consideration of his murals, calling him a gifted primitive. Dealers would offer little churches large sums to take down his walls and sell them as installations to collectors. Maybe some of the churches would refuse to sell, but grow uncomfortable with the secular popularity of the paintings. Still, somewhere there would be a little girl like the girl I had been, a girl who would dream of putting her hand on the cool, sweaty painting while the Son of God blinked down at her in genuine sympathy. Is it a sin, she would wonder, to put together the sacred and the absurd? I would not answer her question, of course. I would leave it, like the art, to make everyone a little nervous and unsure.

I love black-and-white photographs, and I always have. I have cut photographs out of magazines to paste in books of my own, bought albums at yard sales, and kept collections that had one or two images I wanted near me always. Those pictures tell me stories—my own and others, scary stories sometimes, but more often simply everyday stories, what happened in that place at that time to those people. The pictures I collect leave me to puzzle out what I think about it later. Sometimes, I imagine my own life as a series of snapshots taken by some omniscient artist who is just keeping track—not interfering or saying anything, just capturing the moment for me to look back at it again later. The eye of God, as expressed in a Dorothea Lange or Wright Morris. This is the way it is, the photograph says, and I nod my head in appreciation. The power of art is in that nod of appreciation, though sometimes I puzzle nothing out, and the nod is more a shrug. No, I do not understand this one, but I see it. I take it in. I will think about it. If I sit with this image long enough, this story, I have the hope of understanding something I did not understand before. And that, too, is art, the best art.

My friend Jackie used to call my photographs sentimental. I had pinned them up all over the walls of my apartment, and Jackie liked a few of them but thought on the whole they were better suited to being tucked away in a book. On her walls, she had half a dozen bright prints in bottle-cap metal frames, most of them bought from Puerto Rican artists at street sales when she was working as a taxi driver and always had cash in her pockets. I thought her prints garish and told her so when she made fun of my photographs.

"They remind me of my mama," she told me. I had only seen one photograph of Jackie's mother, a wide-faced Italian matron from Queens with thick, black eyebrows and a perpetual squint.

"She liked bright colors?" I asked.

Jackie nodded. "And stuff you could buy on the street. She was always buying stuff off tables on the street, saying that was the best stuff. Best prices. Cheap skirts that lost their dye after a couple of washes, shoes with cardboard insoles, those funky little icons, weeping saints and long-faced Madonnas. She liked stuff to be really colorful. She painted all the ceilings in our apartment red and white. Red-red and white-white. Like blood on bone."

I looked up at my ceiling. The high tin ceiling was uniformly bloody when I moved in, with paint put on so thick, I could chip it off in lumps. I had climbed on stacks of boxes to paint it all cream white and pale blue.

"The Virgin's colors," Jackie told me. "You should put gold roses on the doorposts."

"I'm no artist," I told her.

"I am," Jackie laughed. She took out a pencil and sketched a leafy vine above two of my framed photographs. She was good. It looked as if the frames were pinned to the vine. "I'll do it all," she said, looking at me to see if I was upset.

"Do it," I told her.

Jackie drew lilies and potato vines up the hall while I made tea and admired the details. Around the front door she put the Virgin's roses and curious little circles with crosses entwined in the middle. "It's beautiful," I told her.

"A blessing," she told me. "Like a bit of magic. My mama magic." Her face was so serious, I brought back a dish of salt and water, and we blessed the entrance. "Now the devil will pass you by," she promised me.

I laughed, but almost believed.

For a few months last spring I kept seeing an ad in all the magazines that showed a small child high in the air dropping toward the upraised arms of a waiting figure below. The image was grainy and distant. I could not tell if the child was laughing or crying. The copy at the bottom of the page read: "Your father always caught you."

"Look at this," I insisted the first time I saw the ad. "Will you look at this?"

A friend of mine took the magazine, looked at the ad, and then up into my shocked and horrified face.

"They don't mean it that way," she said.

I looked at the ad again. They didn't mean it that way? They meant it innocently? I shuddered. It was supposed to make you feel safe, maybe make you buy insurance or something. It did not make me feel safe. I dreamed about the picture, and it was not a good dream.

I wonder how many other people see that ad the way I do. I wonder how many other people look at the constant images of happy families and make wry faces at most of them. It's as if all the illustrators have television sitcom imaginations. I do not believe those families. I believe in the exhausted mothers, frightened children, numb and stubborn men. I believe in hard-pressed families, the child huddled in fear with his face hidden, the father and mother confronting each other with their emotions hidden, dispassionate passionate faces, and the unsettling sense of risk in the baby held close to that man's chest. These images make sense to me. They are about the world I know, the stories I tell. When they are accompanied by wry titles or copy that is slightly absurd or unexpected, I grin and know that I will puzzle it out later, sometimes a lot later.

I think that using art to provoke uncertainty is what great writing and inspired images do most brilliantly. Art should provoke more questions than answers and, most of all, should make us think about what we rarely want to think about at all. Sitting down to write a novel, I refuse to consider if my work is seen as difficult or inappropriate or provocative. I choose my subjects to force the congregation to look at what they try so stubbornly to pretend is not happening at all, deliberately combining the horribly serious with the absurd or funny, because I know that if I am to reach my audience I must first seduce their attention and draw them into the world of my imagination. I know that I have to lay out my stories, my difficult people, each story layering on top of the one before it with care and craft, until my audience sees something they had not expected. Frailty—stubborn, human frailty—that is what I work to showcase. The wonder and astonishment of the despised and ignored, that is what I hope to find in art and in the books I write—my secret self, my vulnerable and embattled art, the child I was and the woman I have become, not Jesus at the Jordan but a woman with only her stubborn memories and passionate convictions to redeem her.

"You write such mean stories," a friend once told me. "Raped girls, brutal fathers, faithless mothers, and untrustworthy lovers—meaner than the world really is, don't you think?"

I just looked at her. Meaner than the world really is? No. I thought about showing her the box under my desk where I keep my clippings. Newspaper stories and black-and-white images—the woman who drowned her children, the man who shot first the babies in her arms and then his wife, the teenage boys who led the three-year-old away along the train track, the homeless family recovering from frostbite with their eyes glazed and indifferent while the doctor scowled over their shoulders. The world is meaner than we admit, larger and more astonishing. Strength appears in the most desperate figures, tragedy when we have no reason to expect it. Yes, some of my stories are fearful, but not as cruel as what I see in the world. I believe in redemption, just as I believe in the nobility of the despised, the dignity of the outcast, the intrinsic honor among misfits, pariahs, and queers. Artists—those of us who stand outside the city gates and look back at a society that tries to ignore us—we have an angle of vision denied to whole sectors of the sheltered and indifferent population within. It is our curse and our prize, and for everyone who will tell us our work is mean or fearful or unreal, there is another who will embrace us and say with tears in their eyes how wonderful it is to finally feel as if someone else has seen their truth and shown it in some part as it should be known.

"My story," they say. "You told my story. That is me, mine, us." And it is.

We are not the same. We are a nation of nations. Regions, social classes, economic circumstances, ethical systems, and political convictions—all separate us even as we pretend they do not. Art makes that plain. Those of us who have read the same books, eaten the same kinds of food as children, watched the same television shows, and listened to the same music, we believe ourselves part of the same nation—and we are continually startled to discover that our versions of reality do not match. If we were more the same, would we not see the same thing when we look at a painting? But what is it we see when we look at a work of art? What is it we fear will be revealed? The artist waits for us to say. It does not matter that each of us sees something slightly different. Most of us, confronted with the artist's creation, hesitate, stammer, or politely deflect the question of what it means to us. Even those of us from the same background, same region, same general economic and social class, come to "art" uncertain, suspicious, not wanting to embarrass ourselves by revealing what the work provokes in us. In fact, sometimes we are not sure. If we were to reveal what we see in each painting, sculpture, installation, or little book, we would run the risk of exposing our secret selves, what we know and what we fear we do not know, and of course incidentally what it is we truly fear. Art is the Rorschach test for all of us, the projective hologram of our secret lives. Our emotional and intellectual lives are laid bare. Do you like hologram roses? Big, bold, brightly painted canvases? Representational art? Little boxes with tiny figures posed precisely? Do you dare say what it is you like?

For those of us born into poor and working-class families, these are not simple questions. For those of us who grew up hiding what our home life was like, the fear is omnipresent—particularly when that home life was scarred by physical and emotional violence. We know if we say anything about what we see in a work of art we will reveal more about ourselves than the artist. What do you see in this painting, in that one? I see a little girl, terrified, holding together the torn remnants of her clothing. I see a child, looking back at the mother for help and finding none. I see a mother, bruised and exhausted, unable to look up for help, unable to believe anyone in the world will help her. I see a man with his fists raised, hating himself but making those fists tighter all the time. I see a little girl, uncertain and angry, looking down at her own body with hatred and contempt. I see that all the time, even when no one else sees what I see. I know I am not supposed to mention what it is I see. Perhaps no one else is seeing what I see. If they are, I am pretty sure there is some cryptic covenant that requires that we will not say what we see. Even when looking at an image of a terrified child, we know that to mention why that child might be so frightened would be a breach of social etiquette. The world requires that such children not be mentioned, even when so many of us are looking directly at her.

There seems to be a tacit agreement about what it is not polite to mention, what it is not appropriate to portray. For some of us, that polite behavior is set so deeply we truly do not see what seems outside that tacit agreement. We have lost the imagination for what our real lives have been or continue to be, what happens when we go home and close the door on the outside world. Since so many would like us to never mention anything unsettling anyway, the impulse to be quiet, the impulse to deny and pretend, becomes very strong. But the artist knows all about that impulse. The artist knows that it must be resisted. Art is not meant to be polite, secret, coded, or timid. Art is the sphere in which that impulse to hide and lie is the most dangerous. In art, transgression is holy, revelation a sacrament, and pursuing one's personal truth the only sure validation.

Does it matter if our art is canonized, if we become rich and successful, lauded and admired? Does it make any difference if our pictures become popular, our books made into movies, our creations win awards? What if we are the ones who wind up going from town to town with our notebooks, our dusty boxes of prints or xeroxed sheets of music, never acknowledged, never paid for our work? As artists we know how easily we could become a Flannery O'Connor character, reading those journals of criticism and burying our faces in our hands, staggering under the weight of what we see that the world does not. As artists, we also know that neither worldly praise nor critical disdain will ultimately prove the worth of our work.

Some nights I think of that sweating, girlish Jesus above my mother's determined features, those hands outspread to cast benediction on those giggling uncertain boys, me in the congregation struck full of wonder and love and helpless laughter. If no one else ever wept at that image, I did. I wished the artist who painted that image knew how powerfully it touched me, that after all these years his art still lives inside me. If I can wish for anything for my art, that is what I want—to live in some child forever—and if I can demand anything of other artists, it is that they attempt as much.

Why Jesus Loved Whores

VICKI COVINGTON

Your father is the first to break your heart, and all the others simply fall along the same fault line. You don't learn this, of course, until much later in life. Maybe you find yourself—as I did—in the parking lot of a lowdown café with an architect. He had on cuff links with the insignia of the Episcopal Church. We were in his car, a navy blue Dodge with a CD player. But he wasn't playing CDs. He had the radio on an oldies station. "I Fought the Law" was on. It was almost summer. I hadn't broken a law.

I was married, a mother. We had been inside the café drinking coffee. He was trying to crank up an affair with me, and I'd acquiesced to this point. I had no intentions of having one. I was playing an old game I hadn't played in years, just because I was bored and desperate for excitement and grieving my parents' demise. He mentioned that there was a motel nearby, and I looked down at the table.

"Don't worry," he said, indicating his cuff links. "I actually went to seminary once."

I studied him—the dark eyes, the charming smile. I knew he was a con, or perhaps he was simply trained to spot women like me. Easy marks.

"Did you ever go into the ministry?" I asked.

"No," he replied.

When it was time to go, he paid the $1.50 tab, and I told him I was a cheap date. I'm sure he already knew that. Back in his car, he glanced once more at the motel. The Motel Birmingham. It had been there all my life; its distinguishing characteristic was a plastic woman in a 1950s bathing cap and swimsuit, arched over the marquee in midair, a perfect dive in progress.

"So what happens next?" I asked him.

I have problems with pace, balance, and control. I loved him in the obsessive way I've always loved men. I wanted him to tie me up, bind me. He did, in every sense. And one year later he dumped me so hard I thought I might die.

Some bad girls like bad men. You might get lucky like me and end up marrying a good man. But even then you have a radar for jerks. And jerks are seductive. If their timing is right you can't resist, no matter where you are in life. You can be sixteen or twenty-one or forty-six. Age has nothing to do with it. Young women can count on it haunting them always.

There are many theories of the origin of masochism, but this isn't a scholarly paper. It is an invitation to remember, and women do remember. Our bodies remember.

Which brings us back to the fault line, the place in the internal landscape of our bodies, that vulnerable shifting plate that is irreparable. Most of the time your father put it there—by absence or neglect or abuse or shame or death. But it might have been a big brother who hit you hard or an uncle who loved you so much you let him put his fingers on your lips and maybe in your mouth when you were old enough to know better—say, eighteen. But you let him anyway.

All the boys you date dump you. You beg. You get on your knees on the floorboard. You dial his number, drive by his house, fantasize his apology. You—caught in the drama of the pending earthquake—beseech him: Trample me. Cut the core from me. Re-arrange my tendons, nerve endings, blood cells.

But what if one day that becomes a prayer to God rather than to a man?

Jesus loved whores. He knew the fault line. He saw it as a stripe, like the ones he'd have someday. He dared anyone to cast a stone.

I'm still not completely over the architect who once wanted to be a preacher. I keep thinking that he'll come back unexpectedly like a thief in the night. But he won't, so I go on with life, asking my women friends if they understand this kind of madness.

They do. They all do.

For he was wounded for our transgressions, he was bruised for our iniqui-ties; the chastisement of our peace was upon him: and with his stripes we are healed.

—Isaiah 53:5

Awakening

That's How I Like to See a Woman

SUE MONK KIDD

It was autumn, and everything was turning loose. I was running errands that afternoon. Rain had fallen earlier, but now the sun was out, shining on the tiny beads of water that clung to trees and sidewalks. The whole world seemed red and yellow and rinsed with light. I parked in front of the drugstore where my daughter, Ann, fourteen, had an after-school job. Leaping a puddle, I went inside.

I spotted her right away kneeling on the floor in the toothpaste section, stocking a bottom shelf. I was about to walk over and say hello when I noticed two middle-aged men walking along the aisle toward her. They looked like everybody's father. They had moussed hair, and they wore knit sport shirts the color of Easter eggs, the kind of shirts with tiny alligators sewn at the chest. It was a detail I would remember later as having ironic symbolism.

My daughter did not see them coming. Kneeling on the floor, she was intent on getting the boxes of Crest lined up evenly. The men stopped, peering down at her. One man nudged the other. He said, "Now that's how I like to see a woman — on her knees."

The other man laughed.

Standing in the next aisle, I froze. I watched the expression that crept into my daughter's eyes as she looked up. I watched her chin drop and her hair fall across her face.

Seeing her kneel at these men's feet while they laughed at her subordinate posture pierced me through.

For the previous couple of years I had been in the midst of a tumultuous awakening. I had been struggling to come to terms with my life as a woman—in my culture, my marriage, my faith, my church, and deep inside myself. It was a process not unlike the experience of conception and labor. There had been a moment, many moments really, when truth seized me and I "conceived" myself as woman. Or maybe I reconceived myself. At any rate, it had been extraordinary and surprising to find myself—a conventionally religious woman in my late thirties—suddenly struck pregnant with a new consciousness, with an unfolding new awareness of what it means to be a woman and what it means to be spiritual *as a woman.*

Hard labor had followed. For months I'd inched along, but lately I'd been stuck. I'd awakened enough to know that I couldn't go back to my old way of being a woman, but the fear of going forward was paralyzing. So I'd plodded along, trying to make room for the new consciousness that was unfolding in my life but without really risking change.

I have a friend, a nurse on the obstetrical floor at a hospital, who says that sometimes a woman's labor simply stalls. The contractions grow weak, and the new life, now quite distressed, hangs precariously. The day I walked into the drugstore, I was experiencing something like that. A stalled awakening.

Who knows, I may have stalled interminably if I had not seen my daughter on her knees before those laughing men. I cannot to this day explain why the sight of it hit me so forcibly. But to borrow

Kafka's image, it came like an ice ax upon a frozen sea, and suddenly all my hesitancy was shattered. Just like that.

The men's laughter seemed to go on and on. I felt like a small animal in the road, blinded by the light of a truck, knowing some terrible collision is coming but unable to move. I stared at my daughter on her knees before these men and could not look away. Somehow she seemed more than my daughter; she was my mother, my grandmother, and myself. She was every woman ever born, bent and contained in a small, ageless cameo that bore the truth about "a woman's place."

In the profile of my daughter I saw the suffering of women, the confining of the feminine to places of inferiority, and I experienced a collision of love and pain so great I had to reach for the counter to brace myself.

This posture will not perpetuate itself in her life, I thought.

Still I didn't know what to do. When I was growing up, if my mother had told me once, she'd told me a thousand times, "If you can't say something nice, don't say anything at all." I'd heard this from nearly everybody. It was the kind of thing that got cross-stitched and hung in kitchens all over my native South.

I'd grown up to be a soft-voiced, sweet-mouthed woman who, no matter how assailing the behavior before me or how much I disagreed with it, responded nicely or else ziplocked my mouth shut. I had swallowed enough defiant, disputatious words in my life to fill a shelf of books.

But it occurred to me that if I abandoned my daughter at that moment, if I simply walked away and was silent, the feminine spirit unfolding inside her might also become crouched and silent. Perhaps she would learn the internal posture of being on her knees.

The men with their blithe joke had no idea they had tapped a reservoir of pain and defiance in me. It was rising now, unstoppable by any earthly force.

I walked toward them. "I have something to say to you, and I want you to hear it," I said.

They stopped laughing. Ann looked up.

"This is my daughter," I said, pointing to her, my finger shaking with anger. "You may like to see her and other women on their knees, but we don't belong there. *We don't belong there!*"

Ann rose to her feet. She glanced sideways at me, sheer amazement spread over her face, then turned and faced the men. I could hear her breath rise and fall with her chest as we stood there shoulder to shoulder, staring at their faces.

"Women," one of them said. They walked away, leaving Ann and me staring at each other among the toothpaste and dental floss.

I smiled at her. She smiled back. And though we didn't say a word, more was spoken between us in that moment than perhaps in our whole lives.

I left the drugstore that day so internally jolted by the experience that everything in me began to shift. I sat in the car feeling like a newborn, dangled upside down and slapped.

Throughout my awakening, I'd grown increasingly aware of certain attitudes that existed in our culture, a culture long dominated by men. The men in the drugstore had mirrored one attitude in particular, that of seeking power over another, of staying up by keeping others down.

Sitting in my car replaying my statement back to those men—that women did not belong on their knees—I knew I had uttered my declaration of intent.

That night Ann came to my room. I was sitting in bed reading. She climbed up beside me and said, "Mama, about this afternoon in the drugstore . . . "

"Yeah?"

"I just wanted to say, thanks."

Conceiving the Feminine Self

In "The Archaeology of a Marriage," poet Maxine Kumin wrote, "When Sleeping Beauty wakes up, she is almost fifty years old." I wasn't fifty when my awakening began, but I was nearing forty. I'd lived just long enough for the bottom to start falling out of my notions of womanhood.

It all started when I was thirty-eight, two years before I walked into the drugstore. I was a full-time writer, spending many hours immersed in books. I lived in a nice house with a man I'd been married to for eighteen years, and we had two children, Bob and Ann, both in early adolescence. I went to church regularly and was involved in the social life of the small Southern town where we lived. The last thing I expected was an encounter with feminist spirituality.

Feminist. What a word to deal with. I felt a secret sympathy for the underlying cause of feminism—what it might do for women— but I was uncomfortable with the word, uncomfortable with the images it carried. Overall, I'd kept a discreet distance from it. In fact, if there had been a contest for Least Likely to Become a Feminist, I probably could have made the finals on image alone.

But then one September night, I fell asleep and dreamed a momentous dream:

While sitting on the sand at the edge of the ocean, I am amazed to see that I am nine months pregnant and starting labor. I look around for help, but I am on an island by myself. Well, I think, I'll just have to deliver the baby myself. As the labor begins, I rub my abdomen and breathe deeply. I scoop up water as the waves flow ashore and bathe my abdomen and face. The pain comes and goes. Sometimes I cry and feel I might faint, but then the pain subsides. Finally I start to push. I give birth to a healthy baby girl. I hold her up, laughing with joy. I bring her close and look into her eyes. I am shocked to see I have given birth to myself, that I am the baby and the mother both.

I woke abruptly. You know how some dreams are so vivid you have to spend a few moments after you wake assuring yourself it didn't really happen? That's how I felt, like I needed to look around in the sheets for a newborn. I felt awed, like something of import and worthy of great reverence had taken place.

For years I'd written down my dreams, believing, as I still do, that one of the purest sources of knowledge about our lives comes from the symbols and images deep within. So, being careful not to wake my husband, I slipped out of bed, crept through the darkness into my study, and wrote down the dream.

At breakfast I took my tea to the patio and stared at the morning, wondering about this baby girl who was myself. What new potential did she represent? Who would she grow up to be? The dream was a mystery in many ways, but somehow I knew clearly that it was about my life as a woman.

Despite that realization, it didn't quite sink in that this dream was signaling the beginning of a profound new journey. I didn't know then that the child in the dream would turn my world upside down. That she would eventually change every fundamental relationship in my life: my way of being religious and spiritual, my way of being a woman in the world, my marriage, my career, and my way of relating to other women, to the earth, and even to myself.

At forty (or sometimes thirty or sixty), women grow ripe for feminist spiritual conception. By then we've been around long enough to grow disenchanted with traditional female existence, with the religious experience women have been given to live out.

Nearing forty, I needed to rethink my life as a "man-made woman." To take back my soul. Gradually I began to see what I hadn't seen before, to feel things that until then had never dared to enter my heart. I became aware that as a woman I'd been on my knees my whole life and not really known it. Most of all, I ached for the woman in me who had not yet been born, though I couldn't have told you then the reason for the ache.

When this disenchantment, this ripeness, begins, a woman's task is to conceive herself. If she does, the spark of her awakening is struck. And if she can give that awakening a tiny space in her life, it will develop into a full-blown experience that one day she will want to mark and celebrate.

Conception, labor, and birthing—metaphors thick with the image and experiences of women—offer a body parable of the process of awakening. The parable tells us things we need to know about the way awakening works—the slow, unfolding, sometimes hidden, always expanding nature of it, the inevitable queasiness, the need to nurture and attend to what inhabits us, the uncertainty about the outcome, the fearful knowing that once we bring the new consciousness forth, our lives will never be the same. It tells us that and more.

I've given birth to two children, but bringing them into the world was a breeze compared to birthing myself as woman. Bringing forth a true, instinctual, powerful woman who is rooted in her own feminine center, who honors the sacredness of the feminine, and who speaks the feminine language of her own soul is never easy. Neither is it always welcomed. I discovered that few people will rush over to tie a big pink bow on your mailbox.

Yet there is no place so awake and alive as the edge of becoming. But more than that, birthing the kind of woman who can authentically say, "My soul is my own," and then embody it in her life, her spirituality, and her community is worth the risk and hardship.

Today, eight years after my waking began, I realize that the women who are bringing about this kind of new female life are brand-new beings among us. I keep meeting them; I keep hearing their stories. They confirm my own experience, that somewhere along the course of a woman's life, usually when she has lived just long enough to see through some of the cherished notions of femininity that Culture holds out to her, when she finally lets herself feel the limits and injustices of the female life and admits how her own faith tradition has contributed to that, when she at last stumbles in the dark hole made by the absence of a Divine Feminine presence, then the extraordinary thing I've been telling you about will happen. This woman will become pregnant with herself, with the symbolic female-child who will, if given the chance, grow up to reinvent the woman's life.

This female-child is the new potential we all have to become women grounded in our own souls, women who discover the Sacred Feminine way, women who let loose their strength. In the end we will reinvent not only ourselves, but also religion and spirituality as they have been handed down to us.

Nobel Prize-winning novelist Toni Morrison wrote of her character Pilate in *Song of Solomon* that "when she realized what her situation in the world was . . . she threw away every assumption she had learned and began at zero." With her new awareness, Pilate conceived herself and birthed a new way of being woman.

When my dream came, the potential to do the same rose up. Only it would take a long time to shed my old assumptions and begin at zero.

The Deep Sleep

The dream left me with a vague kind of anticipation, a sense of restlessness. Two things happened as a result. First, I made plans to go away two months later for a solitary retreat at a Benedictine monastery, which I typically did when something was stirring inside. The second thing involved a journal.

Writing is not only my career, it's my compulsion. I keep voluminous journals, normally beginning a new one each January, so it was revealing that soon after the dream, even though it was September, even though I already had a nice journal with months of pages left, I went out and bought a new one. I bought a pink one.

Many mornings throughout October, I sat by the windows in the den before the children awoke, before my husband, Sandy, came in and started the coffee ritual. I sat there thinking about my life as a woman.

So much of it had been spent trying to live up to the stereotypical formula of what a woman should be—the Good Christian Woman, the Good Wife, the Good Mother, the Good Daughter— pursuing those things that have always been held out to women as ideals of femininity.

One morning I wrote about something that had happened several months earlier. I'd been inducted into a group of women known as the Gracious Ladies. I'm not exactly sure what the criteria were, except one needed to portray certain ideals of womanhood, which included being gracious and giving of oneself unselfishly. During a high-lace ceremony, standing backstage waiting to be inducted, I felt a stab of discomfort. I thought about the meticulous way we were coiffed and dressed, the continuous smiling, the charm that fairly dripped off us, the sweet, demure way we behaved, like we were all there to audition for the Emily Post-er Child. We looked like the world's most proper women.

What am I doing here? I thought. Lines from the poem "Warning," by Jenny Joseph, popped into my head and began to recite themselves.

When I am an old woman, I shall wear purple
with a red hat that doesn't go, and doesn't suit me. . . . I shall go out in
   my slippers in the rain
And pick the flowers in other people's gardens
And learn to spit.

from *When I Am an Old Woman I Shall Wear Purple*, ed. Sandra Haldeman Martz

I turned to a woman beside me and said, "After we're Gracious Ladies, does that mean we can't wear purple with a red hat or spit?" She smiled but appeared vaguely dismayed that someone who'd managed to get into the group had just said the word *spit*.

"It's from a poem," I explained.

"I see," she said. Still smiling.

It occurred to me on that October morning that living the female life under the archetype of Gracious Lady narrowed down the scope of it considerably. It scoured away a woman's natural self, all the untamed juices of the female life. It would be many years before I read Clarissa Pinkola Estés's words in *Women Who Run with the Wolves: Myths and Stories of the Wild Woman Archetype,* "When a woman is cut away from her basic source, she is sanitized," but somehow even then, in the most rudimentary way, I was starting to know it.

In my spiritual life I was also a sanitized woman. I had always been very spiritual and very religious, too, so as I wrote in my journal I began trying to put my womanhood together with my spirituality and religion.

I wrote that I was mainstream orthodox. It sounded very dull, but actually it hadn't been dull at all. I'd pursued a spiritual journey of depth and meaning, but—and this was the big realization for me—I'd done so safely within the circle of Christian orthodoxy. I would no more have veered out of that circle than a child would have purposely drawn outside the lines of her coloring book.

I had been raised in the Southern Baptist Church, and I was still a rather exemplary member of one, but beginning in my early thirties I'd become immersed in a journey that was rooted in contemplative spirituality. It was the spirituality of the "church fathers," of the monks I'd come to know as I made regular retreats in their monasteries. I was influenced by Meister Eckhart and Julian of Norwich, who did, now and then, refer to "God our Mother," but this had never really sunk in. It was nice poetry. Now I wondered: What did "God our Mother" really mean?

Morning after morning I wrote, starting to realize how my inner journey had taken me into the airy world of intellect and the fiery realm of spirit, places that suddenly seemed very removed. I thrived on solitude, routinely practicing silent meditation as taught by the monks Basil Pennington and Thomas Keating. Because I visited monasteries and practiced the spirituality they were built upon, people often asked me, "Why do you like monasteries so much?" I would grin and say, "Well, what do you expect? My middle name *is* Monk." Like the Gracious Lady, Monk was an archetype—a guiding inner principle—I lived by.

I'd read many of the classics of Christian contemplative literature, the church fathers and the great mystics of the church. For years I'd studied Thomas Merton, John of the Cross, Augustine, Bernard, Bonaventure, Ignatius, Eckhart, Luther, Teilhard de Chardin, *The Cloud of Unknowing*, and others. Why had it never seemed peculiar that they were all men?

I often went to Catholic mass or Eucharist at the Episcopal church, nourished by the symbol and power of this profound feeding ritual. It never occurred to me how odd it was that women, who have presided over the domain of food and feeding for thousands of years, were historically and routinely barred from presiding over it in a spiritual context. And when the priest held out the host and said, "This is my body, given for you," not once did I recognize that it is women in the act of breast-feeding who most truly embody those words and who are also most excluded from ritually saying them.

When those particular thoughts struck me one morning as I was writing, they pricked a bubble of anger I didn't know I had, and I surprised myself by throwing my pen across the room. It landed inside the fireplace in a pile of soot. I had to go get the pen and clean it off. There had been so many things I hadn't allowed myself to see, because if I fully woke to the truth, then what would I do? How would I be able to reconcile myself to it? The truth may set you free, but first it will shatter the safe, sweet way you live.

The thoughts and memories I was collecting in the journal were random, disjointed. Frankly, I couldn't see what any of them had to do with the dream. It was as if I were walking around and around some secret enclosure, trying to find a way into it. I sometimes wondered what good my pacing was doing.

But after leaving the process for a few days, I would be back in the den, picking up where I'd left off, trying to make sense of things. I wrote about how odd it was that at the same time I was making these retreats in monasteries, going to Eucharist, and meditating on the words of Merton and St. Francis, I was going to a Baptist church—not just on Sunday mornings, but also on Sunday and Wednesday evenings—where the emphasis was not on symbol and silence and God in the soul but on evangelizing and preaching and God in the word. I was a contemplative in an evangelical church, which is sort of like trying to squeeze a round soul into a square slot. It was all I could do to hold the tension between them. I had one foot onshore and the other in a boat that had started to drift.

But despite the inner tension, I kept trying to adapt. The Southern Baptist Church had been the fabric of my religious existence since childhood. And if that wasn't enough, I was married to a Southern Baptist minister who was a religion teacher and chaplain on a Baptist college campus. That alone was enough to keep me securely tethered to the flock. So I taught Sunday school and brought dishes to all manner of potlucks and tried to adjust the things I heard from the pulpit to my increasingly incongruent faith.

I filled pages about my life as a Baptist.

I recorded the time Ann, then eight, tugged on my dress during a church service while the minister was ordaining a new set of deacons. "When are they going to do the women?" she asked.

"The women?" I echoed.

She nodded. Her assumption of equality was earnest and endearing. These days you will find a few female deacons in the more moderate Southern Baptist churches, but not so much then. I'd felt like a harbinger of cruel truth when I told her, "They don't ordain women, honey. Only men."

She had frowned, truly puzzled.

That day in church, the words *only men, only men, only men* went on echoing in my head for a good five minutes, but it soon passed. With a little more ripeness, I might have conceived a new female life that long-ago day, but then I was too consumed with staying in line and being a good and proper woman, something that renders you fairly sterile as far as feminine journeys go.

Writing down that memory reminded me of the time *I* was eight and had my own first encounter with "cruel truth." I was in the churchyard during Vacation Bible School. It was hot. Georgia hot. The girls sat under a tree, making tissue paper corsages, while the boys climbed the limbs above us. I could not remember how it started, only that a quarrel broke out—one of those heated boys-are-better-than-girls or girls-are-better-than-boys arguments that eight-year-olds have with such verve. Finally one of the boys told us to shut up, and, of course, we wanted to know who'd made him our boss. "God!" he said. "God made *us* the boss."

So we girls marched inside to the teacher and asked her point-blank if this was so. We asked her with the same earnest and endearing assumption of equality with which Ann had posed her question to me. And, like me, the teacher was slow to answer. "Well . . . actually . . . technically, I guess I have to say the Bible does make men the head."

"The head?" we asked.

"That means in charge," she said, and looked at us as if to say, "I know, I know, it's a blow, but that's the way it is."

I stared at her, amazed. I had never heard anything like this before, and I was sure it had to be a mistake. A *big* mistake. I mean, if this were true, then women, girls, me—we were not at all what I thought. At eight I couldn't have expressed it fully, but on some level I knew what this meant. That we were less than males and that we were going to spend the rest of our lives obeying and asking permission or worrying if we didn't. That event and others like it would eventually limit everything I ever thought about freedom and dreams and going where they took me. But worse, those events said something about the female gender itself—that it simply wasn't up to par. It had to be subdued, controlled, ruled over.

For girls there is always a moment when the earnest, endearing assumption of equality is lost, and writing about it in my journal thirty years later made me want to take those two eight-year-olds into my arms—myself and Ann, both.

October was nearly spent before I finally got around to reflecting on my life as a "Christian writer," which was how I was often identified. I'd been a prolific contributor to an inspirational magazine with millions of readers. I'd written articles for religious journals and magazines, books about my contemplative spirituality. It always surprised me where my readers turned up. One time I called L. L. Bean to order Sandy a denim shirt, and the operator said she was reading one of my books. I got lots of mail from readers. I spoke at Christian conferences, in churches. As a result, it seemed people expected me to be a certain way. Of course, I expected me to be a certain way, too. And that way had nothing remotely to do with feminist spirituality.

After a month of journal writing, one morning I sat as usual in the den. The light was coming up in the backyard, and the maple, at the height of fall color, appeared to be on fire. As I gazed at it, I understood that while I had gone through a lot of spiritual transformation and written about it, my changes had not deviated much from what were considered safe, standard, accepted Christian tenets. I had never imagined any kind of internal reformation that would call into question the Orthodox Christian Woman, the Good Daughter to the Church, or the Monk who lived high in the spiritual tower of her head. The risk of doing so seemed much too high for lots of reasons, but certainly paramount among them was that it might jeopardize my marriage and my career. I finally came to this:

As a woman, I've been asleep. The knowing rose in me, fast and brilliant, like the light coming now across the grass. I closed the journal and put it away.

A woman in Deep Sleep is one who goes about in an unconscious state. She seems unaware or unfazed by the truth of her own female life, the truth about women in general, the way women and the feminine have been wounded, devalued, and limited within culture, churches, and families. She cannot see the wound or feel the pain. She has never acknowledged, much less confronted, sexism within the church, biblical interpretations, or Christian doctrine. Okay, so women have been largely missing from positions of church power, we've been silenced and relegated to positions of subordination by biblical interpretations and doctrine, and God has been represented to us as exclusively male. So what? The woman in Deep Sleep is oblivious to the psychological and spiritual impact this has had on her. Or maybe she has some awareness of it all but keeps it sequestered nicely in her head, rarely allowing it to move down into her heart or into the politics of her spirituality.

The awarenesses about my female life that emerged during that month were sketchy, thin, and incomplete. A memory here, a thought there, a recognition, an insight—all of them sifting around like vapor. I knew as a woman I'd been asleep, but I had no idea exactly how. I knew I was waking up, but I didn't possess a clue about what I might be waking up to. All I knew was that there was this tiny female life inside, some part of me waking up and wanting to be born. She was rousing me out of years of somnambulance, and something had to be done with her.

The Making of a Preacher's Wife

CASSANDRA KING

I remember the first time the idea came up. I was sixteen, and me and my childhood friend, Leon Ball, were sitting on the sandy banks of the Chattahoochee River, sharing a cigarette. A Camel, unfiltered: I'd stolen it from my daddy's overalls pocket, and bits of tobacco stuck to my tongue when I inhaled, grandly and with much gusto. Actually, I was just learning to inhale; Leon was teaching me. A skinny boy with thick glasses and an infectious giggle, Leon was one of my best buddies, a sort of substitute brother, since I came from a household of sisters.

"Here's what I don't understand about you Methodists," Leon said, squinting through the smoke of the cigarette.

"What?" I asked. Leon belonged to the Baptist church, while I came from generations of Methodists. In the small farming community where he and I were raised in lower Alabama, you were either Baptist, Methodist, or Holiness. I knew some Jewish families from Dothan, the closest town to us, and a couple of highfalutin Episcopalians, but no Catholics. Far as I knew, I'd never seen a real live Catholic.

"It's this—how come every time the Methodists need a *big* Christian to send on one of their retreats or something, they send Sandra King?" Leon asked, and his blue eyes, magnified behind the thick glasses, were playful. Before I could come up with an indignant reply, Leon poked me in the ribs with a sharp elbow and reached for the cigarette. "My turn. You had the last two drags."

I watched with envy as he inhaled expertly, without coughing or sputtering. "It's perfectly obvious why my church sends me on those things," I said, tossing my head. The head toss was a new affectation since I'd turned sixteen and discovered boys. I was already on the tightrope I would walk for the next several years, balancing a Southern Belle, good-little-girl persona with that of an artsy wannabe who smoked cigarettes and dreamed of being a writer.

"Why? Because your mama, your Big Mama, your Aunt Collie Ruth, and your Aunt Thelma run the Methodist church?" Leon asked. Again, I was indignant, but he was right about one thing: although we didn't know the term then, the influential women in my life were all church ladies, leaders in our church, every last one of them.

"Bull. I was just elected a youth delegate for the *whole* state of Alabama, and they had nothing to do with that," I reminded him, apparently not too concerned about the deadly sin of pride. "Give me that cigarette. You're the one hogging it now."

Only a stub was left, and I had to hold it carefully with my fingertips to keep from burning myself, an art that pot smokers would perfect in the following years. I could feel Leon's eyes on me as I put the cigarette out in the white sand of the riverbank. "What?" I asked him.

"I just don't get it, is all," he said. "How come you smoke and drink beer if you're such a big Christian, always running around going to those Methodist things?"

"You think I'll go to hell?" I was joking, but Leon's slight frown made me realize he wasn't. In the Baptist denomination, many such activities were disapproved of. Why don't Baptists have sex standing up, I'd recently asked Leon, then answered my own question: because people might think they're dancing. I'd laughed at my own humor (I often crack myself up), but Leon had merely rolled his eyes.

"Your mama would have a hissy fit if she knew you were learning to smoke a cigarette, wouldn't she?" Leon persisted, and I nodded. In our day and age, Leon *had* to smoke to be cool, even if he might go to hell as a result, but nice young Southern ladies did not do so.

"Don't worry about me going to hell, Leon," I said, lying on the sandy bank, my hands behind my head. "I might just marry me a preacher. It would make my mama and aunts and everyone at the church happy, and then I'd be in real good with God."

Leon laughed so hard he fell over beside me and kept laughing till I punched his shoulder and told him to shut up. "YOU a preacher's wife," he hooted, removing his glasses and wiping his eyes. "That'll be the day! I got a better chance of becoming a preacher than you have of marrying one, girl. God would faint and fall off his throne if that ever happened."

As far as I know, Leon Ball never became a preacher, and God has yet to faint and fall off his throne. But I ended up spending more than two decades as a preacher's wife, something that still surprises me, years later.

Yet it shouldn't come as such a shock, I suppose. Even though the Methodists were considered more liberal, more lax in interpreting the Bible and Christian propriety than the other denominations I grew up around, the household I was raised in was a fairly pious one. In the Southern rural family of my day and age, religion played a major role. The Methodist Church was the primary focus of the King family's spiritual and social life, as it was with all my relatives and friends. As a matter of fact, from the day I was born until the day I left the church almost five decades later, the Methodist Church was one of the most influential components of my life.

When Sunday morning came, no one in my family ever said, "Are we going to church today?" Never. We went. I didn't think anything about it; it was just something we did. We went to Sunday school every Sunday, and we stayed for the morning worship service afterward. Occasionally some of my friends got to "miss church," which meant go home after Sunday School, but I never did. I knew better than to ask. My mother sang in the choir, and my sisters and I, dressed in stiffly starched dresses my mother had made and smocked by hand, sat with my daddy and grandparents in the King pew. Like most of the men in the congregation, my daddy and granddaddy dozed during the sermon, which was affectionately tolerated by their attentive wives, sitting ramrod straight, eyes on the preacher. But if my little sisters and I giggled or squirmed or didn't pay attention, we got in trouble. Unlike some of the kids with more tolerant parents, we weren't allowed to color or draw pictures on the church bulletin. Because I was a few years older than my little sisters, Rebecca and Nancy Jane, I was in charge of them, responsible for their behavior as well as mine. Another of my responsibilities was to give my daddy an urgent prod if he fell so sound asleep that he started snoring. Until I was eighteen years old and left for college, I spent every morning worship service sitting watchfully between my two playful little sisters but within easy reach of my daddy, a notoriously loud snorer. All this was under the eagle eye of my mother, monitoring our behavior from her perch in the choir loft.

Because our mother was in the choir, I was the one to take the youngest, Nancy Jane, to her first Communion, after she turned three and had to go to "big church" rather than stay in the nursery during the service. On that particular Sunday, Daddy had stayed home with my other sister, Rebecca, who was sick, so it was just me and Nancy Jane. When we knelt at the altar, I showed Nancy Jane how to take the wafer and eat it, then drink the tiny shot glass of grape juice, removing it firmly from her grip when she stuck her tongue in to get the last drop. Proudly, I led my little sister back to the pew, while the congregation beamed on me, the dutiful big sister. But I was to learn that pride goeth before a fall. When we resumed our seats, I noticed that Nancy Jane had the Communion wafer gripped tightly in her chubby little hand. "Nancy Jane," I gasped in a whisper. "You were supposed to eat that." The body of Jesus, I thought in horror; my little sister has the body of Jesus squished up in her hand.

"I ain't eating that piece of paper," Nancy Jane said in a loud voice, and the whole church got quiet. "I'm not a billy goat!"

It started with a giggle behind me, then the whole congregation burst into laughter. I was so mortified I could feel my face burning, and when I dared raise my eyes to the choir, my mother and aunts were staring down at me in disapproval. King children did not disrupt church services, and I had disgraced the family by allowing it to happen.

Every Sunday after a big dinner of fried chicken or roast beef or baked ham (lunch, actually; we had dinner at noon and supper in the evening), my parents read the Sunday paper and took a nap to rest up for the church services yet to come. Sunday was a high holy day, with a hushed and reverent atmosphere about it, since no one worked (women's work, washing dishes and cleaning up the kitchen, didn't count), cut the grass (never on a Sunday!), or even fed the farm animals (they were given extra portions Saturday night to tide them over). At six o'clock, we drove back into town for Methodist Youth Fellowship and Sunday evening services. Midweek we returned to the church again, for prayer meeting and choir practice, and often during the week, for Sunday school parties or potluck suppers. Another duty of mine was to keep my sisters occupied while our mother was at choir practice. I was particularly diligent in this because I didn't want either of them to suffer the same fate I had. When I was four years old, I'd gotten a spanking in front of God and everybody because my mother had told me to sit quietly in the pew until choir practice was over. Instead, I started doing cartwheels down the aisle, which might not have gotten me in so much trouble except for one thing: in order to get more comfortable, I'd removed my shoes, socks, and panties. I'm pretty sure that I'm the only person in the Methodist church to have mooned an entire choir. Years later, I'm still trying to find a metaphor there.

Brought up the way I was, the lifestyle of the preacher's wife fit me like the snow-white gloves my sisters and I wore with our new bonnets and dresses on Easter Sundays. Although it might surprise me now that I spent so many years in that role, I have to admit that I was raised for it. I see now that the same way some young *ladies* are carefully educated and trained to be corporate wives and helpmates for their husbands-to-be in a future life, I was groomed by the formidable church ladies—my mother, my grandmother, and my aunts—to be the perfect little preacher's wife.

Unless Freud is correct and there are no accidents, I became a preacher's wife by accident, sort of. Although my new husband was in theology school, he promised me he didn't intend to pastor a church, that he was perfectly content with his position coaching and running a youth program at a YMCA in Atlanta. For a couple of years, it looked like I was going to have it all, married to a preacher-man as well as keeping God, Leon, and the church ladies happy. But one fateful day I was told to start packing—the preacher-man had just accepted an appointment at a church in Alabama. (Women's lib hadn't taken hold in the South in the early seventies, even in progressive Atlanta. Evidently discussing this plan with me first never entered the picture.) One day I was living in a cozy, green-shuttered house in Buckhead, and a few days later, in a pristine parsonage in Tuscaloosa, Alabama.

After the initial shock wore off, instead of rebelling against my fate, I settled down to become the kind of preacher's wife I had been raised to be. My mother and aunts and the rest of the church ladies swung into operation, full attack mode, supplying me with everything I needed to make it: casserole recipes, devotional books, housekeeping tips, and advice on getting along with the parsonage committee and the bishop's wife. I followed their advice dutifully, and for several years, I was the darling of the church set. My mother couldn't have been prouder than she was the day I was elected vice president of the powerful organization of preacher's wives, the Susies. By the way, I still find it ironic that the Susies were named after Susannah Wesley, who was the mother of John Wesley, the founder of the Methodist Church, instead of being called after his poor nameless wife, whoever she was. By all appearances, God was in his kingdom, and all was right with my world. As long as I didn't stop long enough to question my life, as long as I refused to listen to an inner voice that cried *who am I and what am I doing here,* everything went well, and everyone was happy.

During those seemingly joy-filled years, I was haunted by a terrifying dream that began to occur more and more frequently. I would wake up gasping for breath, my heart pounding, from a dream in which a black cloth was placed over my face, and I couldn't breathe until I fought it off. Talk about a metaphor! It would be many years later before I'd see my first burka, but I felt a cold chill of recognition when I did. I knew I was losing my identity, lost in the role I was playing, but I didn't know what to do about it. Where was the young woman who sat on the banks of the Chattahoochee River with Leon Ball, smoking forbidden cigarettes and exploring questions of religion and propriety and damnation? Was Leon wrong to acknowledge her existence, to laugh at the idea of her leading a life of piety? And where was the young woman who dreamed of being a writer, who spent so much time closed away in her room, making up stories and plays and poems? Oh, I was still writing, but that too had become a convention, like the rest of my life. I wrote devotionals and religious poems and church pageants, not out of devotion and true piety, but to please and impress others.

Something else was going on, too. During my years as a preacher's wife, I played the role I was born to play, and my mother and the other church ladies who had molded me to do so nodded their approval. I'm sure they never suspected that I was empty inside, that the spirituality that had always been a strong part of my makeup had begun to die, smothered by the strictures and conventions of my life. Like the dream cloth placed over my face, the persona I developed had very effectively covered over and buried the questioning, curious part of me. The busy work of serving God had replaced the search for Him, a quest I had embarked on many years ago, when I first asked the ageless questions about life and death and the meaning of it all. At one point, I sought out a minister I respected, someone whose preaching spoke to me and seemed relevant to the questions I had and the mounting panic I was feeling.

"I can't do this anymore," I said to him, my voice breaking. "Everybody thinks I'm something I'm not. I've *become* something I'm not! I'm beginning to feel alone and lost. Please help me." I couldn't bring myself to tell him that I was also terrified and in utter despair because somewhere along the way, I had not only lost myself, I had lost God.

"Now, now, honey," he said to me, "you're doing a fine job. Everybody enjoys the little plays you put on, and the programs you write for the women's groups, and those sweet devotionals and poems you've published. God has given you a gift as a writer, and you're using it for His glory. So go on back to the parsonage and keep writing. Tell you what, why don't you do an Easter meditation for the bulletin next week?"

Crushed, I thanked him and left his office. But in the end, I took his advice. I did as he suggested. However, I no longer wrote Christmas pageants and plays for the youth groups and programs for the women's circles. Instead, I started to write for myself, in secret. I began to describe in a journal my struggles to fill the role I felt so uncomfortable in, and I also started a novel about a woman like myself, a preacher's wife who questions not only her life but also her relationship with her husband, her church, and her God. When I told my preacher-husband that I was writing a novel, he suggested I spend my time more wisely with the church and family. Once a source of pride for both of us, my writing became a source of conflict instead. A writer has to have solitude for introspection, something not available when life is lived in a goldfish bowl. A writer needs a room or at the very least a corner of a room that is apart from the demands of a family, a spouse, and a church, and my struggles to claim this space heightened the tension to an unbearable level. As a result, I went further and further underground with my writing. My marriage was falling apart, but my novel was taking shape.

Although it would be many years after I'd left my time as a preacher's wife before my novel saw the light of day, I can see now that the writing of it was my salvation. At one time, I'd found salvation in the church and in the orderly conventions of worship and ritual; now it came to me in other ways. The act of writing about the despair I felt helped to ease that despair. In my writings, I came to realize that I hadn't lost God; I'd merely misplaced Him/Her. Like the popular song, I had been looking for love in all the wrong places. While I could still find meaning in the beautiful, ancient rituals of the church as well as solidarity in a *koinonia* of believers, God, as I understood the concept, wasn't limited to ritual and convention or to liturgical spaces. To find God, I had to fling the church doors open and run outside.

Long before it was hammered into me that God lived in a big white house with a steeple and stained glass in the windows, I sought a spiritual connection in the sand and water and wind and trees, the moon and the stars. Although I was raised in the church, I was—first and foremost—raised on a farm, a product of the black dirt and sandy soil and red clay of south Alabama. As a child, I spent my days roaming the fields and swinging from grapevines and eating wild blackberries and scuppernongs. Growing up on a farm, I learned birdsongs and the seasons and growing cycles. I held a cane fishing pole before I held a hymnal, and I could catch a fish before I could read the Bible. Before I could repeat the Apostle's Creed by rote, I knew the legend of the dogwood and the story of the crucifixion as revealed in the skeleton of a crab. As a child, spending summers in Florida taught me to love the coast in the same way I loved the farm. It was there I found that God also existed in the waves and sea and wide expanse of the sky. Although I was too young to understand that I came from the earth and I would return to it, that knowledge came to me over time. I began to see that God is in everything, and all of us—man, woman, animal, tree, plant, sand, sea—are made of the same particles. As Whitman said, "I bequeath myself to the dirt to grow from the grass I love, / If you want me again look for me under your boot-soles."

My mama and the rest of the church ladies have long since died, gone on to walk the streets of gold and dwell in heavenly mansions, to don wings and wear halos and play their harps for all eternity. I hope they have fellowship suppers in heaven so they can still make their deviled eggs and pound cakes and casseroles. I hope heaven has an active altar guild as well as all sorts of committees, especially the pastor–parish relations and parsonage and worship committees. Surely God and the archangels need their halos shined and their feathers fluffed; the heavenly Sunday schools still need teachers; and the angels have to have choir practice in order to perfect their hallelujahs. But here's the main thing: When the church ladies peek over the edge and look down on this sinful world, I hope they won't spot me, the ex-preacher's wife, hiding from them, crouched over my computer as I write this. But if they do, I hope they will forgive me for failing to be one of them. It wasn't because I didn't try.

Knowing Our Place

BARBARA KINGSOLVER

I have places where all my stories begin.

One is a log cabin in a deep, wooded hollow at the end of Walker Mountain. This stoic little log house leans noticeably uphill, just as half the tobacco barns do in this rural part of Southern Appalachia, where even gravity seems to have fled for better work in the city. Our cabin was built of chestnut logs in the late 1930s, when the American chestnut blight ran roughshod through every forest from Maine to Alabama, felling mammoth trees more extravagantly than the crosscut saw. Those of us who'll never get to see the spreading crown of an American chestnut have come to understand this blight as one of the great natural tragedies in our continent's history. But the pragmatic homesteaders who lived in this hollow at that time simply looked up and saw a godsend. They harnessed their mule and dragged the fallen soldiers down off the mountain to build their home.

Now it's mine. Between May and August, my family and I happily settle our lives inside its knobby, listing walls. We pace the floorboards of its porch while rain pummels the tin roof and slides off the steeply pitched eaves in a limpid sheet. I love this rain; my

soul hankers for it. Through a curtain of it I watch the tulip poplars grow. When it stops, I listen to the woodblock concerto of
dripping leaves and the first indignant Carolina wrens reclaim-
ing their damp territories. Then come the wood thrushes, heart-
breakers, with their minor-keyed harmonies as resonant as poetry.
A narrow beam of sun files between the steep mountains, and
butterflies traverse this column of light, from top to bottom to top
again, like fish in a tall aquarium. My daughters hazard the damp
grass to go hunt box turtles and crayfish, or climb into the barn
loft to inhale the scent of decades-old tobacco. That particular
dusty sweetness, among all other odors that exist, invokes the most
reliable nostalgia for my own childhood; I'm slightly envious and
have half a mind to run after the girls with my own stick for poking
into crawdad holes. But mostly I am glad to watch them claim my
own best secrets for themselves.

On a given day I may walk the half mile down our hollow to
the mailbox, hail our neighbors, and exchange a farmer's evaluation of the weather (*terrible;* it truly is always either too wet or too
dry in these marginal tobacco bottoms). I'll hear news of a house
mysteriously put up for sale, a dog on the loose, or a memorable
yard sale. My neighbors use the diphthong-rich vowels of the hill
accent that was my own first language. My great-grandfather grew
up in the next valley over from this one, but I didn't even know
that I had returned to my ancestral home when I first came to visit.
After I met, fell in love with, and married the man who was working this land, and agreed to share his home as he also shares mine
in a distant place, I learned that I have close relatives buried all
through these hollows. Unaccustomed as I am to encountering
others with my unusual surname, I was startled to hear neighbors in this valley say, "Why, used to be you couldn't hardly walk
around here without stepping on a Kingsolver." Something I can
never explain, or even fully understand, pulled me back here.

Now I am mostly known around these parts by whichever of my relatives the older people still remember (one of them, my grandfather's uncle, was a physician who, in the early 1900s, attended nearly every birth in this county requiring a doctor's presence). Or else I'm known as the gal married to that young fella that fixed up the old Smyth cabin. We are suspected of being hard up (the cabin is quite small and rustic for a family of four) or a little deranged; neither alternative prevents our being sociably and heartily welcomed. I am nowhere more at home than here, among spare economies and extravagant yard sales glinting with jewel-toned canning jars.

But even so, I love to keep to our hollow. Hard up or deranged I may be, but I know my place, and sometimes I go for days with no worldly exchanges beyond my walk to the mailbox and a regular evening visit on our favorite neighbor's porch swing. Otherwise I'm content to listen for the communiqués of pileated woodpeckers, who stay hidden deep in the woods but hammer elaborately back and forth on their hollow trees like the talking drummers of Africa. Sometimes I stand on the porch and just stare, transfixed, at a mountainside that offers up more shades of green than a dictionary has words. Or else I step out with a hand trowel to tend the few relics of Mrs. Smyth's garden that have survived her: a June apple, a straggling, etiolated choir of August lilies nearly shaded out by the encroaching woods, and one heroic wisteria that has climbed hundreds of feet into the trees. I try to imagine the life of this woman who grew corn on a steeper slope than most people would be willing to climb on foot, and who still, at day's end, needed to plant her August lilies.

I take walks in the woods, I hang out our laundry, I read stories to my younger child, I hike down the hollow to a sunnier spot where I look after the garden that feeds us. And most of all, I write. I work in a rocking chair on the porch, or at a small blue desk facing the window. I write a good deal by hand, on paper, which—I somehow can't ever forget—is made from the macerated hearts of fallen trees.

The rest of the year, from school's opening day in autumn till its joyful release in May, I work at a computer on a broad oak desk by a different window, where the view is very different but also remarkable. In this house, which my predecessors constructed not from trees (which are scarce in the desert Southwest) but of sun-baked mud (which is not), we nestle into what's called in this region a *bosque*—that is, a narrow riparian woodland stitched like a green ribbon through the pink and tan quilt of the Arizona desert. The dominant trees are mesquite and cottonwood, with their contrasting personalities: the former swarthy with a Napoleonic stature and confidence, the latter tall and apprehensive, trembling at the first rumor of wind. Along with Mexican elder, buttonwillow, and bamboo, the mesquites and cottonwoods grow densely along a creek, creating a shady green glen that is stretched long and thin. Picture the rich Nile valley crossing the Saharan sands, and you will understand the fecundity of this place. Picture the air hose connecting a diver's lips to the oxygen tank, and you will begin to grasp the urgency. A riparian woodland, if it remains unbroken, provides a corridor through which a horde of fierce or delicate creatures may prowl, flutter, swim, or hop from the mountains down through the desert and back again. Many that follow this path—willow flycatchers, Apache trout—can live nowhere else on earth. An ill-placed dam, well, ranch, or subdivision could permanently end the existence of their kind.

I tread lightly here, with my heart in my throat, like a kid who's stumbled onto the great forbidden presence (maybe sex, maybe an orchestra rehearsal) of a more mature world. If I breathe, they'll know I'm here. From the window of my study I bear witness to a small, tunnelish clearing in the woods, shaded by overarching mesquite boughs and carpeted with wildflowers. Looming over this intimate foreground are mountains whose purple crowns rise to an altitude of nine thousand feet above the Tucson basin. In midwinter they often wear snow on their heads. In fall and early spring, blue-gray storms draw up into their canyons, throwing parts of the strange topography into high relief. Nearer at hand, deer and jackrabbits and javelina halt briefly to browse my clearing, then amble on up the corridor of forest. On insomniac nights I huddle in the small glow of my desk lamp, sometimes pausing the clicking of my keys to listen for great horned owls out there in the dark, or the ghostly, spine-chilling rasp of a barn owl on the hunt. By day, vermilion flycatchers and western tanagers flash their reds and yellows in the top of my tall window, snagging my attention whenever they dance into the part of my eyesight where color vision begins. A roadrunner drops from a tree to the windowsill, dashes across the window's full length, drops to the ground, and moves on, every single day, running this course as smoothly as a toy train on a track. White-winged doves feed and fledge their broods outside just inches from my desk, oblivious to my labors, preoccupied with their own.

One day not long ago I had to pull myself out of my writerly trance, having become aware of a presence over my left shoulder. I turned my head slowly to meet the gaze of an adolescent bobcat at my window. Whether he meant to be the first to read the story on my computer screen or was lured in by his own reflection in the quirky afternoon light, I can't say. I can tell you, though, that I looked straight into bronze-colored bobcat eyes and held my breath, for longer than I knew I could. After two moments (his and mine) that were surely not equal—for a predator must often pass hours without an eyeblink, while a human can grow restless inside ten seconds—we broke eye contact. He turned and minced away languidly, tail end flicking, for all the world a cat. I presume that he returned to the routine conjectures and risks and remembered scents that make up his bobcat-life, and I returned to mine, mostly. But some part of my brain drifted after him for the rest of the day, stalking the taste of dove, examining a predator's patience from the inside.

It's a grand distraction, this window of mine. "Beauty and grace are performed," writes Annie Dillard, "whether or not we will or sense them. The least we can do is try to be there." I agree, and tend to work where the light is good. This window is *the world* opening onto me. I find I don't look out so much as *it* pours in.

What I mean to say is, I have come to depend on these places where I live and work. I've grown accustomed to looking up from the page and letting my eyes relax on a landscape upon which no human artifact intrudes. No steel, pavement, or streetlights, no architecture lovely or otherwise, no works of public art or private enterprise—no hominid agenda. I consider myself lucky beyond words to be able to go to work every morning with something like a wilderness at my elbow. In the way of so-called worldly things, I can't seem to muster a desire for cellular phones or cable TV or to drive anything flashier than a dirt-colored sedan older than the combined ages of my children. My tastes are much more extreme: I want wood-thrush poetry. I want mountains.

It would not be quite right to say I *have* these things. The places where I write aren't actually mine. In some file drawer we do have mortgages and deeds, pieces of paper (made of dead trees—mostly pine, I should think), which satisfy me in the same way that the wren yammering his territorial song from my rain gutter has satisfied himself that all is right in *his* world. I have my ostensible claim, but the truth is, these places own *me:* They hold my history, my passions, and my capacity for honest work. I find I do my best thinking when I am looking out over a clean plank of planet earth. Evidently I need this starting point—the world as it appeared be-

fore people bent it to their myriad plans—from which to begin
dreaming up my own myriad, imaginary hominid agendas.

And that is exactly what I do: I create imagined lives. I write
about people, mostly, and the things they contrive to do for, against,
or with one another. I write about the likes of liberty, equality, and
world peace, on an extremely domestic scale. I don't necessarily
write about wilderness in general or about these two places that I
happen to love in particular. Several summers ago on the cabin
porch, surrounded by summertime yard sales and tobacco auc-
tions, I wrote about *Africa,* for heaven's sake. I wrote long and hard
and well until I ended each day panting and exhilarated, like a
marathon runner. I wrote about a faraway place that I once knew
well, long ago, and I have visited more recently on research trips,
and whose history and particulars I read about in books until I
dreamed in the language of elephants. I didn't need to *be* in Africa
as I wrote that book; I needed only to be someplace where I could
think straight, remember, and properly invent. I needed the blessed
emptiness of mind that comes from birdsong and dripping trees. I
needed to sleep at night in a square box made of chestnut trees who
died of natural causes.

It is widely rumored, and also true, that I wrote my first novel in a
closet. Before I get all rapturous and carried away here, I had better
admit to that. The house was tiny, I was up late at night typing
while another person slept, and there just wasn't any other place
for me to go but that closet. The circumstances were extreme. And
if I have to—if the Furies should take my freedom or my sight—I'll
go back to writing in the dark. Fish gotta swim, birds gotta fly,
writers will go to stupefying lengths to get the infernal roar of
words out of their skulls and onto paper. Probably I've already

tempted fate by announcing that I need to look upon wilderness in order to write. (I can hear those Furies sharpening their knives now, clucking, *Which shall it be, dearie? Penury or cataracts?*) Let me back up and say that I am breathless with gratitude for the collisions of choice and luck that have resulted in my being able to work under the full-on gaze of mountains and animate beauty. It's a privilege to live any part of one's life in proximity to nature. It is a privilege, apparently, even to know that nature is out there at all. In the summer of 1996 human habitation on earth made a subtle, uncelebrated passage from being mostly rural to being mostly urban. More than half of all humans now live in cities. The natural habitat of our species, then, officially, is steel, pavement, streetlights, architecture, and enterprise—the hominid agenda.

With all due respect for the wondrous ways people have invented to amuse themselves and one another on paved surfaces, I find that this exodus from the land makes me unspeakably sad. I think of the children who will never know, intuitively, that a flower is a plant's way of making love, or what *silence* sounds like, or that trees breathe out what we breathe in. I think of the astonished neighbor children who huddled around my husband in his tiny backyard garden, in the city where he lived years ago, clapping their hands to their mouths in pure dismay at seeing him pull *carrots* from the *ground*. (Ever the thoughtful teacher, he explained about fruits and roots and asked, "What other foods do you think might grow in the ground?" They knit their brows, conferred, and offered brightly, "Spaghetti?") I wonder what it will mean for people to forget that food, like rain, is not a product but a process. I wonder how they will imagine the infinite when they have never seen how the stars fill a dark night sky. I wonder how I can explain why a wood-thrush song makes my chest hurt to a populace for whom wood is a construction material and thrush is a tongue disease.

What we lose in our great human exodus from the land is a rooted sense, as deep and intangible as religious faith, of why we need to hold on to the wild and beautiful places that once surrounded us. We seem to succumb so easily to the prevailing human tendency to pave such places over, build subdivisions upon them, and name them The Willows, or Peregrine's Roost, or Elk Meadows, after whatever it was that got killed there. Apparently it's hard for us humans to doubt, even for a minute, that this program of plunking down our edifices at regular intervals over the entire landmass of planet earth is overall a good idea. To attempt to slow or change the program is a tall order.

Barry Lopez writes that if we hope to succeed in the endeavor of protecting natures other than our own, "it will require that we reimagine our lives. . . . It will require of many of us a humanity we've not yet mustered, and a grace we were not aware we desired until we had tasted it."

And yet no endeavor could be more crucial at this moment. Protecting the land that once provided us with our genesis may turn out to be the only real story there is for us. The land *still* provides our genesis, however we might like to forget that our food comes from dank, muddy earth, that the oxygen in our lungs was recently inside a leaf, and that every newspaper or book we may pick up (including this one, ultimately, though recycled) is made from the hearts of trees that died for the sake of our imagined lives. What you hold in your hands right now, beneath these words, is consecrated air and time and sunlight and, first of all, a place. Whether we are leaving it or coming into it, it's *here* that matters, it is place. Whether we understand where we are or don't, that is the story: To be *here* or not to be. Storytelling is as old as our need to remember where the water is, where the best food grows, where we find our courage for the hunt. It's as persistent as our desire to teach our children how to live in this place that we have known longer than they have. Our greatest and smallest explanations for ourselves grow from place, as surely as carrots grow in the dirt. I'm presuming to tell you something that I could not prove rationally but instead feel as a religious faith. I can't believe otherwise.

A world is looking over my shoulder as I write these words; my censors are bobcats and mountains. I have a place from which to tell my stories. So do you, I expect. We sing the song of our home because we are animals, and an animal is no better or wiser or safer than its habitat and its food chain. Among the greatest of all gifts is to know our place.

Oh, how can I say this: People *need* wild places. Whether or not we think we do, we *do*. We need to be able to taste grace and know once again that we desire it. We need to experience a landscape that is timeless, whose agenda moves at the pace of speciation and glaciers. To be surrounded by a singing, mating, howling commotion of other species, all of which love their lives as much as we do ours, and none of which could possibly care less about our economic status or our running day calendar. Wildness puts us in our place. It reminds us that our plans are small and somewhat absurd. It reminds us why, in those cases in which our plans might influence many future generations, we ought to choose carefully. Looking out on a clean plank of planet earth, we can get shaken right down to the bone by the bronze-eyed possibility of lives that are not our own.

Relics of Summer

FRANCES MAYES

The fonts in all the churches are dry. I run my fingers through the dusty scallops of marble: not a drop for my hot forehead. The Tuscan July heat is invasive to the body but not to the stone churches that hold on to the dampness of winter, releasing a gray coolness slowly throughout the summer. I have a feeling, walking into one, then another, that I walk into palpable silence. A lid seems to descend on our voices, or a large damp hand. In the vast church of San Biago below Montepulciano, there is an airy quiet as you enter. Right under the dome, you can stand in one spot and speak or clap your hands and far up against the inner cup of the dome an eerie echo sends the sound rapidly back. The quality of the sound is not like the hello across a lake but a sharp, repeated return. Your voice flattened, otherworldly. It is hard to think a mocking angel isn't hovering against the frescoes, though more likely a pigeon rests there.

Since I have been spending summers in Cortona, the major shock and joy is how at home I feel. But not just at home, returned to that primal first awareness of home. I feel at home because dusty trucks park at intersections and sell watermelons. The same thump to test for ripeness. The boy holds up a rusty iron scale with discs of different sizes for counterweight. His arm muscle jumps up like Popeye's and the breeze brings me a whiff of his scent of dry grasses, onions, and dirt. In big storms, lightning drives a jagged stake into the ground and hailstones bounce in the yard, bringing back the smell of ozone to me from Georgia days when I'd gather a bowlful the size of Ping-Pong balls and put them in the freezer.

Sunday is cemetery day here, and though our small-town Southern plots are austere compared to these lavish displays of flowers on almost every grave, we, too, made Sunday pilgrimages to Evergreen with glads or zinnias. I sat in the backseat, balancing the cool teal vase between my knees while my mother complained that Hazel never turned her hand to pick one stem and it was her own mother lying there, not just a mother-in-law. Gathered around Anselmo Arnaldo, 1904–1982, perhaps these families are saying, as mine did, Thank God the old goat's lying here rather than still driving us crazy.

Sweltering nights, the air comes close to body temp, and shifting constellations of fireflies compete with stars. Mosquito nights, grabbing at air, the mosquito caught in my hair. Long days when I can taste the sun. I move through this foreign house I've acquired as though my real ancestors left their presences in these rooms. As though this were the place I always came home to.

Living near a small town again certainly is part of it. And living again with nature. (A student of mine from Los Angeles visited. When I walked him out to the end of the point for the wide-angle view of lake, chestnut forests, Apennines, olive groves, and valleys, he was unprepared. He stood silently, the first time I'd known he could, and finally said, "It's, uh, like nature.") Right, nature: Clouds swarm in from over the lake and thunder cracks along my backbone, booms like waves boom far out at sea. I write in my notebook: "The dishwasher was struck. We heard the sizzle. But isn't it good, the gigantic storm, the flood of terror they felt beside fires in the cave? The thunder shakes me like a kitten the big cat has picked up by the neck. I ricochet home, heat lightning; I'm lying on the ground four thousand miles from here, letting rain soak through me."

Rain flays the grapes. Nature: What's ripe, will the driveway wash away, when to dig potatoes, how much water is in the irrigation well? Early life reconnects. I go out to get wood; a black scorpion scuttles over my hand and suddenly I remember the furry tarantulas in the shower at Lakemont, the shriek when my barefooted mother stepped on one and felt it crunch, then squash up soft as a banana between her toes.

Is it the spill of free days? I dream my mother rinses my tangle of hair with a bowl of rainwater.

Sweet time, exaggerated days, getting up at dawn because when the midsummer sun tops the crests across the valley, the first rays hit me in the face like they strike some rock at Stonehenge on the solstice. To be fully awake when the sky turns rose-streaked coral and scarves of fog drift across the valley and the wild canaries sing. In Georgia, my father and I used to get up to walk the beach at sunrise. At home in San Francisco what wakes me is the alarm at seven, or the car pool horn blowing for the child downstairs, or the recycle truck with its crashing cascade of glass. I love the city and never have felt really at home there.

I was drawn to the surface of Italy for its perched towns, the food, language, and art. I was pulled also to its sense of lived life, the coexistence of times that somehow gives an aura of timelessness —I toast the Etruscan wall above us with my coffee every morning— all the big abstracts that act out in everything from the aggression on the *autostrada* to the afternoon stroll through the piazza. I cast my lot here for a few short months a year because my curiosity for the layered culture of the country is inexhaustible. But the umbilical that is totally unexpected and elides logic reaches to me through the church.

To my surprise I have bought a ceramic Mary with a small cup for home use of holy water. As a fallen-away Methodist, then a fallen-away Episcopalian, I suppose my holy water is a sham. However, I have taken it from the spring I discovered near the house, the artesian spring where clear water rises in a declivity of white stone. This looks like holy water to me. It must have been the house's original source. Or it's older than the house—medieval, Roman, Etruscan. Though some interior juggling is going on, I do not expect to emerge as a Catholic, or even as a believer. I am essentially pagan by birth. Southern populism was boiled into my blood early; the idea of a pope with the last word gives me hives. "Idolatrous," our minister called the worship of Mary and the saints. "Mackerel snapper," my classmates teased Andy Evans, the lone Catholic in our school. Briefly, in college, I was drawn to the romance of the Mass, especially the three a.m. fishermen's Mass in St. Louis Cathedral in New Orleans. I lost interest in the whole show when my good friend, a New Orleans Catholic, told me in complete seriousness that mortal sin began if you kissed longer than ten seconds. A ten-second French kiss was OK, but a dry twenty-second kiss would land you in trouble. Though I still like rituals, even empty ones, what magnetizes me here feels more radical.

Now I love the quick Mass in tiny upper Cortona churches, where the same sounds have provided a still point for the residents for almost eight hundred years. When a black Labrador wandered in, the priest interrupted his holy spiel to shout, "For the love of God, somebody get that dog out of here." If I stop in on a weekday morning, I sit there alone, enjoying the country Baroque. I think: Here I am. I love the parade of relics through the streets, with gold-robed priests travelling along in a billow of incense, their

way prepared by children in white, scattering the streets with petals of broom, rose, daisy. In the noon heat, I almost hallucinate.
What's in the gold box held aloft with banners—a splinter from
the cradle? Never mind we thought Jesus was born in a lowly man-
ger; this is the splinter of the true cradle. Or am I confused? It's
a splinter of the true cross. It is on its way through the streets,
brought out into the air one day a year. And suddenly I think,
What did that hymn mean, *cleft for me,* rising years ago, perpendicular from the white board church in Georgia?

In my South, there were signs on trees that said "Repent." Halfway up a skinny pine, up beyond the tin trough that caught the
resin, hung a warning, "Jesus is coming." Here, when I turn on the
car radio, a lulling voice implores Mary to intercede for us in purgatory. In a nearby town, one church has as its relic a phial of Holy
Milk. As my student would say, that's from, like, Mary.

On the terrace at noon, I'm tanning my legs as I read about early
martyrs and medieval saints. I'm drawn to the martyred San Lorenzo, who was put on a grill for his troublesome faith and seared
until he reportedly said, "Turn me over, I'm done on this side,"
and thereby became the favorite saint of chefs. The virginal young
women martyrs all were raped, stabbed, tortured or locked away
because of their devotion to Christ. Sometimes the hand of God
reached down and swept one away, like Ursula, who did not wish
to marry the barbarian Conan. With her ten thousand virgins (all
avoiding men?) loaded into boats, she was lifted miraculously by
God and sailed across the unfriendly skies, then deposited in Rome,
where they all bathed in lime-scented water and formed a sacred
order. Stunning, the prevalence of the miracle. In the Middle Ages,
some of the venerated women found the foreskin of Jesus materi-

alized in their mouths. I don't know if there exists a relic of that. (Would it look like a chewed rubber band? A dried wad of bubble gum?) The foreskin stops me for a good ten minutes and I stare out at the bees swarming the *tigli* trees, trying to imagine that event happening, and not just once. The moment of recognition, what she said, what the reaction was—a boggling speculation. Somehow, I'd never heard of these kinkier saints in America, although someone once sent me a box of new books, each one about a saint's life. When I called the bookstore, they told me my benefactor wished to remain anonymous. Now I read on and find that some had "holy anorexia" and lived on the wafer alone. If a saint's bones were dug up, a flowery fragrance filled the town. After Saint Francis preached to the birds, they flew up into the shape of a cross then separated into the four directions. The saints would eat the pus and lice of the poor to show their humility; in turn, the faithful liked to drink the bathwater of a holy person. If, after death, a saint's heart was cut out, perhaps an image of the Holy Family carved in a ruby would be found inside. *Oh*, I realize, *here's where they put their awe.* I understand that.

I understand because this everyday wildness and wonder come back so naturally from the miracle-hungry South. They almost seem like memories somehow, the vertebrae of the Virgin, the toenail of San Marco. My favorite, the breath of San Giuseppe, foster father of Christ. I imagine an opaque green glass bottle with a ground stopper, the swift exhaling of air as it opened. At home when I was small, our seamstress kept her jar of gallstones on the windowsill above her Singer. Marking my hem, her mouth full of pins, she'd say, "Lord, I don't want to go through nothing like that again. Now you turn round. Those things won't even dissolve in gasoline." Her talisman against sickness. Emblems and omens.

Santa Dorotea immured in her cell for two years, against a high-walled pit in the dank cathedral. Communion through a grate and a diet of bread and gruel. I hated visiting Miss Tibby, who treated the corns on my mother's little toes, shaving yellow curls of skin off with a vegetable peeler, then rubbing her feet with thick lotion that smelled like crank case oil and Ovaltine. The bare bulb lit not only my mother's foot on a cushion but also a coffin where Miss Tibby slept at night so there would be no surprises later.

In high school my friends and I parked a block away and secretly peered in the windows of the Holy Rollers, who spoke in tongues, sometimes screaming with a frightening ecstatic look on their faces and falling to the floor writhing and jerking. We were profane, smothering our laughter at the surely sexual fervor and the contorted postures. Later we'd sit in the car, Jeff smoking, and watch them file out of the peeling church, looking as normal as anyone. In Naples, the phial of San Gennaro's congealed blood liquifies once a year. There's also a crucifix that used to grow one long hair of Jesus that would have to be barbered once a year. That one seems particularly close to Southern sensibilities.

In the United States, I think there is no sanctioned place to put such fixated strangeness so it just jumps out when it has to. Driving through the South recently, I stopped near Metter, Georgia, for a barbecue sandwich. After the sweet salty pork and iced tea, I was directed out back to the bathroom by the owner; pork-bellied, sweating over his pit, he merely nodded toward the rear. No sign at all that as I opened the screen door I would encounter two molting ostriches. How they came to be in that remote town in south Georgia and what iconographical necessity led the family to gaze on and house these dusty creatures is a philosophical gift I've been given to ponder in nights of insomnia.

Growing up in the God-fearing, faith-healing, end-of-the-world-is-at-hand South gave me many chances to visit snake collections beside gas stations when my parents stopped to fill up; to drive past roadside religious ceremonies in which snakes were ecstatically "handled"; to see shabby wonders-of-the-world exhibits—reliquaries of sorts—in the towns bordering the swamps. I know a box of black cat's bones makes a powerful conjure. And that a bracelet of dimes can ward it off. I was used to cages of baby alligators crawling on the back of the mother of all, a fourteen-foot beauty who opened her jaws wide enough that I could have stood in them. The sagging chicken-wire fences couldn't save you if those sleeping logs rose up and decided to take off after you—alligators can run seventy miles an hour. Albino deer covered with ticks that leapt on my hand when I petted their mossy noses, a stuffed painter (panther) with green marbles for eyes, a thirty-foot tapeworm in a jar. The owner explains that it was taken from the throat of his seventeen-year-old niece when the doctor lured it out of her stomach with a clove of garlic on a toothpick. They waited until it showed its head, lured it out further, then grabbed, chopped off its head with a straight razor while hauling the thing out of Darleen's stomach like a rope out of the river.

Wonders. Miracles. In cities, we're less and less capable of the imagination for the superreal, ground down as we are by reality. In rural areas, close to the stars and groves, we're still willing to give it a whirl. So I recover the cobra, too, so much more impressive with his flattened head than rattlesnakes, whose skins paper the office of the owner of the Eighth Wonder of the World, where we have stopped for gas at the Georgia border. We are close to Jasper, Florida, where my mother and father were married in the middle of the night. I am amazed, despite my mother's warning that the owners are carnival people and it is not worth seeing and I have exactly ten minutes or they will go on to White Springs without me. The slight thrill at the possibility of being left behind on this curve of road lined with moss-draped oaks, the silver-bullet trailer set up on concrete blocks, a woman glimpsed inside, washing her hair over a tin bowl and the radio blaring "I'm So Lonesome I Could Cry." I knew then and still know that the man with the phosphorescent glow-in-the-dark torch tattooed on his back and the full-blown roses tattooed on his biceps believed his wonders were real. I follow him to the bamboo hut, where the cobra from darkest Calcutta rises to the song made by blowing on a comb covered with cellophane. The cobra mesmerizes the mangy dog thumping his tail in the doorway. The peacock gives a powerful hee-haw, shakes himself into full regalia, the blues in his fan of feathers more intense than my own or my mother's eyes, and, as everyone knows, we have the purest sky-blue eyes. The peacock's eyes look exactly like the snake's. The owner's wife comes out of the trailer with a boa constrictor casually draped around her neck. She checks on another snake, to whom she has fed a large rat without even cutting it up. The rat is simply disappearing, like a fist into a sweater sleeve. I buy a Nehi and an oatmeal cookie sandwich, run out to the Oldsmobile vibrating in the heat. My father scratches off; gravel spumes behind us. "What have you got?" My mother turns around.

"Just a cold drink and this." I hold up the large cookie.

"Those things have lard in the middle. That's not icing—that's pure-T lard with enough powdered sugar to make your teeth crack."

I don't believe her but when I break open the cookie, it is crawling with maggots. I quickly throw it out the window.

"What did you see in that awful gyp joint?"

"Nothing," I answer.

Growing up, I absorbed the Southern obsession with place, and place can seem to me somehow an extension of the self. If I am made of red clay and black river water and white sand and moss, that seems natural to me.

However, living as a grown woman in San Francisco, I never

have that belonging sensation. The white city with its clean light on the water, the pure, heart-stopping coast, and the Marin hills with the soft contours of sleeping giants under blankets of green— I am the awed tourist, delighted to have made this brief escape, which is my adult life. My house is just one of thousands; my life could be just another story in the naked city. My eye looks with insouciance at the scissors point of the Transamerica pyramid and jagged skyline I can see from my dining room window. Everyone seems to have cracked the door two inches to see who's there. I see you through my two inches; you see me through yours. We are monumentally self-reliant.

I never tire of going into Italian churches. The vaulted arches and triptychs, yes. But each one also has its characteristic blue dust smell, the smell of time. The codified Annunciations, Nativities, and Crucifixions dominate all churches. At the core, these all struggle with the mystery of the two elementals—birth and death. We are frangible. In the side altars, the high arches, the glass manuscript cases in the crypts, the shadowed curves of the apse, these archetypal concerns and the dreamland of religious fervor lock horns with the painterly subject matter in individualized ways. I'm drawn to a bizarre painting that practically leaps off the wall. In a dark, high panel close to the ceiling in San Gimignano, there's Eve rising boldly out of supine Adam's open side. Not the *whoosh* of instantaneous creation I've imagined from reading Genesis, when she appeared as easily as "Let there be Light." This is graphic, someone's passion to be *present* at the miracle. As graphic as the wondrous cobra of Calcutta spiraling up in the humid air of south Georgia before my very eyes. Adam is meat. The vision grabs the viewer like the glow-in-the-dark torch. Now hear this, loud and clear. In Orvieto's Duomo, Signorelli's humans, just restored to their flesh on Judgment Day, stand grandly and luxuriously beside the grinning skeletons they were just moments before. Parts of the body still glow with the aura of the bare bone, a gauzy white light emanating from the firm, new flesh in its glory. A strange turn—we're used to thinking of the decay of the flesh; here's the dream of rejuvenation. Flitting around in the same arena of that cathedral are depictions of hell, green-headed devils with snaky genitals. The damned are twisted, poked, jabbed, while one voluptuous blonde (no doubt what *her* sins were) flies away on the back of a devil with stunted, unaerodynamic wings. Clearly we are in someone's head, midnight imaginings of the descent, the fall, the upward turn. The paintings can be sublime but there is a comic book aspect to much church painting, a wordless progression of blunt narrative very close to those of fire-and-brimstone fundamentalists who still hold forth in the South. If there was more than one word, *Repent,* hanging on those Southern pines, it was bound to be *Doomsday.*

Wandering around in churches, I see over and over San Sebastiano pierced with arrows, martyred Agata holding out her breasts on a plate like two over-easy eggs, Sant'Agnes kneeling piously while a lovely youth stabs her in the neck. Almost every church has its locked relic box like a miniature mausoleum, and what does this mean? Thorn from the crown. Finger digits of San Lorenzo. The talismans that say to the viewers, "Hold on; like these, have faith." Standing in the dim crypt in a country church where a handful of dust has been venerated for several hundred years, I see that even today, toward the end of the century, the case is remembered with fresh carnations. I uncover my second realization: *This is where they put their memories and wants.* Besides functioning as vast cultural repositories, these churches map intimate human needs. How familial they begin to seem (and how far away from the historical church, the bloody history of the Papacy): the coarse robe of St. Francis, another phial of Mary's, this one filled with tears. I see them like the locket I had, with a curl of light brown hair, no one remembered whose, the box of rose petals on the closet shelf behind the blue Milk of Magnesia bottle and the letters tied with frayed ribbon, the translucent white rock from Half Moon Bay. *Never forget.* As I wax the floor tiles and wring out the mop, I can think of Santa Zita of Lucca, saint of housekeeping, as was Willie Bell Smith in my family's house. Basketmaker, beggar, funeral director, dysentery sufferer, notary, speleologist— everyone has a paradigm. *I once was lost but now I'm found.* The medieval notion that the world reflects the mind of God has tilted in my mind. Instead, the church I perceive is a relief map of the human mind. A thoroughly secular interpretation: that we have created the church out of our longing, memory, out of craving, and out of the folds of our private wonders.

If I have a sore throat from drinking orange juice when I know I'm allergic to it, the saint is there in his monumental church at Montepulciano, that town whose syllables sound like plucked strings on the cello. San Biago is a transubstantiated metaphor and a handful of dust in a wrought box. Its small keyhole reminds us of what we most want to be reminded of, *you are not out there alone.* San Biago focuses my thoughts and throws me beyond the scratchy rawness of my own throat. *Pray for me, Biago, you are taking me farther than I go.* When the TV is out of whack and the buttons won't improve the picture, nor will slapping the side soundly, Santa Chiara is out here somewhere in saintland. *Chiara,* clear. She was clairvoyant and from there is only a skip and jump to *receiver,* to patron saint of telecommunications. So practical for such a transcendent girl. A statue of her on top of the TV won't hurt a thing. Next year on July 31, the wedding ring of Mary will be displayed in the Duomo in Perugia. The history says it was "piously stolen" — isn't that an oxymoron — from a church in Chiusi. Without a shred of literal belief, I, for one, will be there.

❧

At the top of the stairs, I touch the springwater in my ceramic Mary with my fingertip and make a circle on my forehead. When I was baptized, the Methodist minister dipped a rose in a silver bowl of water and sprinkled my hair. I always wished I'd been baptized standing knee deep in the muddy Alapaha, held under until the last moment of breath then raised to the singing congregation. My springwater in Mary's cup is not transformed to wash away my sins or those of the world. She always seems like *Mary,* the name of my favorite aunt, rather than Santa Maria. Mary simply became a friend, friend of mothers who suffered their children's pain, friend of children who watched their mothers suffer. She's hanging over almost every cash register, bank teller, shot giver, bread baker in this town, and I've grown used to her presence. The English writer Tim Parks says that without her ubiquitous image to remind you that all will go on as before, "you might imagine that what was happening to you here and now was unique and desperately important . . . I find myself wondering if the Madonna doesn't have some quality in common with the moon." Yes. My unblessed water soothes. I pause at the top of the stairs and repeat the lovely word *acqua.* Years ago, the baby learned to say *acqua* on the lakeshore at Princeton, under a canopy of trees blooming madly with pink pompons. *Acqua, acqua,* she shouted, scooping up water and letting it rain on her head. *Acqua* sounds closer to the sparkle and fall, closer to wetness and discovery. Her voice still reverberates but now I touch my little finger as I remember. The gold signet ring, a family treasure, slipped off in the grass that day and was not to be found. *Water of life. Intimacy of memory.*

Intimacy. The feeling of touching the earth as Eve touched it, when nothing separated her.

In paintings, the hilltop town rests in the palm of Mary's hand or under the shelter of her blue cloak. I can walk every street of my Georgia town in my mind. I know the forks in the pecan trees, the glut of water in the culverts, the hog pear in the alley. Often the Tuscan perched villages seem like large castles—extended homes with streets narrow as corridors, and the *piazze,* like public reception rooms, teeming with visitors. The village churches have an attitude of privacy; the pressed linen and lace altar cloths and scarlet dahlias in a jar could be in family chapels; the individual houses, just suites in the big house. I expand, as when my grandparents' house, my aunt's, my friends', the walls of home were as familiar to me as the lines in my own palm. I like the twisted streets up to the convent where I may leave a bit of lace to be mended on a Catherine wheel, spin it in to the invisible nun, whose sisters have tatted in this great arm of the castle for four hundred years. I do not glimpse even the half moons of her nails or the shadow of her habit. Outside two women who must have known each other all their lives sit in old wooden chairs between their doorways and knit. The stony street slopes abruptly down to the town wall. Beyond that stretches the broad valley floor. Here comes a miniature Fiat up this ridiculously steep street no car should climb. Crazy. My father would drive through swollen streams that flooded sudden dips in the dirt roads. I was thrilled. While he laughed and blew the horn, water rose around the car windows. Or was the water really that high?

We can return to live in these great houses, unbar the gates, simply turn an immense iron key in the lock and push open the door.

From Birmingham to Redemption

DIANE McWHORTER

My uncle referred to our family as "the Whiskeypalian McWhorters" —even though we were Presbyterians. That was partly to distinguish us suave Birmingham McWhorters from our teetotaling Methodist cousins in the north Alabama piney woods. But it's true that when as an adult I encouraged a friend who had moved to Birmingham from Montgomery to join my church, she said with contempt, "Those aren't real Presbyterians. They're Presbyterians who think they're Episcopalians." Indeed, though the Episcopal church is typically the pastoral microbase of a given community's mega-elite, the heavenly host to the titans of my hometown was Independent Presbyterian.

Besides being the heavy manufacturing mecca of Dixie, the proud Pittsburgh of the South, Birmingham was also known as the most segregated city in America at the time I was growing up there in the 1960s. The white church's role in that distinction may be inferred from the response I had come up with to the great moral question of sixth grade: "Are you prejudice?" (We meant "prejudiced," but apparently didn't know the word could be a verb.) Back then I was a classic specimen of the white status quo, a young girl growing up "over the mountain" that separated us from the less privileged residents of our city in a valley. Most of my classmates looked pained and confessed that they were prejudice, but I had come up with a finely nuanced compromise. "I'm a white supremacist," I said, "but I'm not *prejudice* against them." I really thought that it was possible to be part of a barbaric social order without being mean or uncharitable in the Christian sense. And that was the position of most of Birmingham's white churches back then: Make evil nice.

The Presbyterians had a special hedge against moral accountability. Besides "Are you prejudice?" the other burning question of the schoolyard was "Do you believe in predestination?" (Now I should note that neither of these questions was as important as: "Are you for Alabama or Auburn?", "Do you belong to the Birmingham Country Club or the Mountain Brook Club?", and "Are you double-jointed?") The subject of predestination has never come up in my own daughters' peer group (though somehow the double-jointed debate continues, and it turns out that everyone is still double-jointed, just as every young girl claims an "olive complexion" in those multiple-choice beauty quizzes). But during my childhood, predestination was a question about which everyone I knew had an opinion by first grade.

The reason was this: Because it was the most industrial city in the South, Birmingham was arguably the most class-conscious as well. The gap between the employing class and their employees was ruthlessly maintained, and it explains why the favored denomination of the reigning industrialists (they were known as "Big Mules") was Presbyterianism. Put in blunt terms, predestination —the notion that one is "elected" for damnation or salvation— made the Big Mules feel that they had been divinely ordained to make money and, in the process, to treat their workers as chattel. Just as the industrialists were chosen for their glorious destiny, so had the laborers been consigned by God to a purgatory on earth.

These dynamics were acted out rather dramatically in the founding of my church back in 1916 and in its plucky christening as "Independent" in a city insistent on conformity. At the high-toned South Highland Presbyterian Church downtown, the most powerful deacon was a big heresy hunter named James Bowron, a fundamentalist interpreter of the Scripture who regularly ran off ministers if they refused to affirm, for example, that Jonah had literally lived in the belly of the whale. Bowron was not a Bible-thumping Southerner but a bushy-bearded Englishman, who had been one of the founders of the Tennessee Coal and Iron Company. The name notwithstanding, TCI (as the company was known) was the big industrial player in Birmingham, by then the huge Southern fiefdom of the U.S. Steel Corporation. Back in the nineteenth century and well into the twentieth, TCI was among the leading proponents of a sort of post–Civil War slave-labor system known as the convict lease, under which the state hired out its prisoners to industrialists to work in the coal mines. Many of the convicts had committed crimes no more serious than gambling, indebtedness, or idleness. "Lazy" workers were literally crucified, though tied rather than nailed to the cross. Fugitives were tracked by bloodhounds and given a lashing. Those who were beaten to death were dumped, along with the many convicts who contracted and died of tuberculosis, into a common hole in the woods. Such was the temporal kingdom created by the devoutest deacon at Birmingham's South Highland Presbyterian Church.

Two South Highland pastors had already met Deacon Bowron's fatal disfavor by the time the man who went on to found my church crossed him. He was Henry Edmonds, a product of small-town Alabama and a militant practitioner of the social gospel that ministered to the victims of industrialization—like his deacon's employees. Social gospel men did not believe in predestination, but Edmonds also rejected almost every other key doctrine of the church. He did not believe in original sin or the virgin birth or that Christ had died for our sins, and he didn't much care whether or not He had risen from the dead. But that wasn't what upset the heresy-hunting Bowron most. His main beef was that Edmonds challenged the "imperfectible" conditions—meaning the social inequities—that supported Birmingham's economy. Bowron blasted Edmonds (and this has got to be one of the most remarkable bits of reasoning in the history of the church) for "trying to improve relations between husband and wife, between classes, nations, races. We ought to rejoice if those relations grow worse and worse for when they become intolerable Christ will come again." In other words, the pious deacon contended that the sins he had committed against his fellow man in the course of his day job were a good thing, because they were going to lead to the millennium.

A few months into the controversy, on October 23, 1916, Edmonds resigned. There was nothing remarkable in that; opinions like his would have gotten one branded as a Communist atheist in societies less conservative than Birmingham. What was amazing was that 450 of the wealthiest church members—the biggest of the Big Mules—left South Highland with Edmonds, and stood by him when the Southern Presbytery stripped him of his credentials. The new church he formed, Independent Presbyterian, became the most powerful and (with perhaps one or two small, Episcopal exceptions) the snootiest congregation in the city. When Edmonds needed a country house to recuperate from an illness, the president of U.S. Steel's TCI—he was my Whiskeypalian uncle's grandfather-in-law—gave him a plot of company land to build it on. U.S. Steel's local lawyer, Walker Percy, the namesake grandfather of the great novelist, had also been one of Edmonds's main loyalists. My grandfather, a big lawyer for the Alabama Power Company, joined the church with his new bride in the early 1920s.

Despite a congregation seemingly so at odds with his ministry, Edmonds refused to be domesticated. In the 1920s, an estimated half of Birmingham's Protestant clergy were members of the Ku Klux Klan, and most of the other half, as one put it, had a high regard for the Klan's principles even if they didn't always agree with its methods. Edmonds was alone among Birmingham's Protestant clergy in crusading publicly against the anti-Catholicism that was the Klan's calling card at the time. Friends posted armed guards at a local theater where he condemned the entire community for the acquittal of a Klansman who had assassinated the city's leading Catholic priest. (A dazzling local trial lawyer named Hugo Black had been the murderer's successful attorney. How Black, whose political career was launched by the Klan, went on to be one of the most vigorous liberals on the Supreme Court is another Birmingham spiritual odyssey.)

In the 1930s, Edmonds led the local fight to free the Scottsboro Boys, the black youths railroaded to death sentences on false charges of raping two white women. He became so frustrated with the intransigence of the Alabama justice system that he finally, incredibly, pledged cooperation with the American Communist Party, which had seized control of the Scottsboro defense as its first propaganda splash and turned the case into an international cause célèbre. And then, fearless amid the anti-red hysteria, Edmonds began speaking out for black suffrage.

How could a man with views like this have been one of the most esteemed and even beloved figures in a city known as the Johannesburg of America—a city that was the exemplar of what Franklin Roosevelt had called the "latent fascism" of the South? I think that exceptional men like him were essential to the moral hygiene of their communities. In a benighted time and place, men like Edmonds are tolerated, indeed praised, because they are the last, tenuous connections to the better angels of our nature—the term Abraham Lincoln used at Gettysburg to grasp at the hope that some good, some renewal of American purpose, would come of the carnage from that first epic conflict over class and race. They were what enabled an immoral society to live with itself.

Like everything else in my town, the socially transformative power of Christianity observed segregation. The religion's revolutionary "meek-shall-inherit-the-earth" spirit bore the sign "Colored." The black church produced the civil rights movement that put Birmingham on the map. In the spring of 1963, Martin Luther King Jr. and Birmingham's own Reverend Fred Shuttlesworth led those biblical demonstrations, with schoolchildren facing down police dogs and fire hoses, that broke the back of segregation in America. On Good Friday, King had gotten himself arrested for marching, and he used the opportunity to write his landmark treatise on nonviolence, "Letter from Birmingham Jail." The letter, which became one of the sacred texts of our democracy, was addressed rhetorically to eight local white clergymen who had asked him to get out of town.

By the time Martin Luther King arrived, Birmingham's great Presbyterian, Henry Edmonds, had retired from the pulpit, and his legacy was sorely missing from my Christian education. Independent Presbyterian imparted to me a sense of the beauty and the mystery of religion, so that today I cannot sing "Holy, Holy, Holy" without choking up. But the church was not what transformed me from the white supremacist girl I was in 1963 to the person writing this today.

I found religion in history, though it turned out I did owe my epiphany to Jesus. As a child I never was able to understand His struggle, say, when He was being tempted by the devil. I didn't see why He didn't just use his Son of God superpowers to deflect Satan's tricks. And every time I revisited the Crucifixion on Good Friday, I would root for Jesus to pull out a miracle for Himself— vault from the cross and throw a few nonviolent punches at His tormenters. I mark the beginning of my spiritual maturity from the time I realized that Jesus would not have been Christ if He had not died on the cross.

Robert Penn Warren described this acceptance of one's destiny as "identifying with fate." I identified with fate when I confronted the history of my city and plumbed the mysterious process by which I, as a Sunday school girl in 1963, could feel no empathy for the four black girls, also precious to Jesus' sight, who were killed by Klan dynamite in a church across town on a Sunday morning that September. Murdering the innocents is, of course, as old as the Bible. So it was in the spirit of a religious quest that I would spend the better part of my adulthood trying to figure out how the ordinary churchgoers of my time and place deformed their consciences to support a form of genocide.

The result was my book *Carry Me Home*, and at the end I think I finally learned the meaning of redemption: I understood how my Magic City, so nicknamed by the shameless booster who founded Birmingham, and the Tragic City it seemed destined to be were one and the same. John Coltrane captured that tension in a piece he recorded two months after the Birmingham church bombing. The song, "Alabama," inspired (if that is the right word) by that cataclysm, is "a frightening emotional portrait of some place, in these musicians' feelings," the playwright then known as LeRoi Jones wrote in the album's liner notes. "If that 'real' Alabama was the catalyst, more power to it, and may it be this beautiful, even in its destruction."

I love the sly double meaning of "destruction," for it touches the gnarly, paradoxical way we human beings arrive at truth and meaning. Which I guess are my version of God. And so the last lines of *Carry Me Home* celebrate the unintended gift of my hometown: The most segregated U.S. city gave us one of the glorious achievements of the civil rights movement. "Birmingham was America's city in a valley, but out of the depths rose a city upon a hill. Beauty from destruction. There is magic in that."

Full Circle

PAULI MURRAY

Renee's death changed my life. It was more than the loss of a close friend. In Renee's dying hours I had come face to face with my own mortality. I felt an urgency to complete my mission on earth in the days left to me. From its beginnings, our friendship had centered around the church, and it was in the church that I had found the comforting belief that the living and the dead are bound together in the "communion of saints." For the second time in my life I had been called upon to *be with* a devout Christian whom I loved in the crisis of death and to minister in ways I associated only with the ordained clergy. As I reflected upon these experiences, the thought of ordination became unavoidable. Yet the notion of a "call" was so astounding when it burst into my consciousness that I went about in a daze, unable to eat or sleep as I struggled against it.

In spite of my vigorous advocacy of women's ordination in the Episcopal Church as a matter of principle, my age and, more important, my sense of unworthiness had insulated me against entertaining such a possibility for myself. It had taken a cataclysm, watching my friend in an abyss of suffering, to force my submission and obedience to Divine Will. Now that Will seemed to be leading me into the unknown, on a journey that demanded utmost faith and trust.

In my indecision, I went to the Reverend Alvin L. Kershaw of Emmanuel Church in Boston, which I had begun to attend. After several conversations he assured me I was on the right track. "You and your friend Renee were engaged in a Christian ministry," I remember him saying. "Now that she is gone, you can carry it on for both."

Once I admitted the call of total commitment to service in the church, it seemed that I had been pointed in this direction all my life and that my experiences were merely preparation for this calling. In spite of my own intellectual doubts and the opposition to women's ordination that was widespread within the Episcopal Church at the time, I took the fateful step of applying to the Right Reverend John M. Burgess, bishop of the Diocese of Massachusetts, for admission to holy orders.

In due course Bishop Burgess turned me over to Suffragan Bishop Morris F. Arnold, who supervised candidates for ordination in the diocese. Bishop Arnold put me at ease in our first session by telling me about his maiden speech in the House of Bishops a year earlier during a debate on women's ordination. He had forthrightly told his brethren that the Second Coming of Christ would not necessarily be represented by someone of the same sex or the same race as the First Coming. Bishop Arnold's sympathetic support was a bulwark of strength in the rugged days that followed. In June 1973, when I was accepted as a postulant from the Diocese of Massachusetts, supporters of women's ordination to the priesthood were optimistic that the triennial General Convention meeting at Louisville that fall would approve this historic change in Anglican tradition. In September, however—by which time I had resigned from Brandeis, moved to New York, and entered the Gen-

eral Theological Seminary for a year of training as a special student—
the organized opposition had become more vocal and advocates of
women's ordination were less hopeful. I had barely begun my studies when the convention met and voted the issue down.

The convention's rebuff left women seminarians as well as women
who were already ordained deacons with an uncertain future in
the church. This continuing barrier had especially serious implica-
tions for me as I approached my sixty-third birthday. Having given
up my academic career and the financial security it provided, I
would be severely handicapped by my age in seeking professional
employment after my year of training was completed. No official
action would be taken by the church for another three years, when
the General Convention would meet again; meanwhile I would be
in limbo. To avoid this untenable position (and despite the fact that
my academic background did not require me to complete addi-
tional formal study), I petitioned the faculty to change my status
to that of a regular three-year student and a candidate for the master of divinity degree.

Those three years of seminary subjected me to the most rigorous discipline I had ever encountered, surpassing by far the rig-
ors of my law school training. For most people, I think, seminary
is an intensely intellectual and emotional experience of living with
others in close quarters while dealing with imponderables and
the ambiguities of human existence. It brings to the surface hidden doubts about religious faith as well as fears, insecurities, and
unresolved problems. One's personality is under the continuous
scrutiny of instructors and schoolmates as well as under constant
self-examination. In addition to daily devotions and corporate
worship, seminarians have to absorb an immense body of learning.
Throughout the process they have to satisfy various layers of the
church hierarchy not only that they are academically competent

but also that the spiritual formation essential to a priestly calling is plainly evident in their bearing.

Women seminarians were in a peculiarly ambiguous position in the mid-1970s. Although we were formally accepted as candidates for a degree and for ordination to the diaconate, we were the center of bitter controversy, the targets of veiled and sometimes overt hostility. Our numbers were few and our presence in a community designed for men only was more tolerated than encouraged. The admission of women to the General Theological Seminary was so recent that the first two women to graduate received their degrees at the end of my first year there. My own situation was especially complex. Not only was I the only Negro woman enrolled, but I felt set apart because I was the oldest student in residence, senior in age and professional experience to most of my professors and several decades older than my classmates, most of whom were white and male and in their twenties, only a few years older than the students I had taught at Brandeis. My legal training was a mixed blessing; while it contributed to clarity of expression, my forensic approach was disturbing in a theological setting. My natural tendency to probe and debate an issue collided with some of the instructors' concepts of being "pastoral," and I soon got a reputation for being "abrasive," a view some professors, believing such a character trait would hinder my ministry, insisted upon expressing in my evaluation report at the end of my first year.

Another complaint, which almost wrecked my seminary career that first year, was that I was "rude" and cut people off in the middle of a sentence when they were speaking in class. I was appalled by this accusation but was at a loss to explain myself until my friend Page Smith Bigelow, a senior, accidentally discovered the real trouble when she borrowed tapes I had recorded in a theology course. After listening to several tapes, Page came to me and said, "Pauli, you are cutting people off because you don't hear them when they drop their voices at the end of a sentence." Tests confirmed that I had a serious hearing loss in both ears, and the deficiency was partially corrected through appliances attached to my eyeglasses. The difference was amazing. With the hearing aids I heard sounds I had not been aware of for years, but I soon learned why so many people who have hearing aids consider them an abomination. The appliances are not yet sensitive enough to tune out background noise, so that turning up the volume to listen to someone speaking magnifies other sounds to a harsh, confusing clatter.

Given my volatile temperament, it was providential that I did not go to the General Convention of 1973. I was too new a postulant to risk a rebuff at the outset of the long road to ordination. By not going I was less battered than the women who went with such fervent hope. This became evident when I attended a weekend conference of women seminarians and deacons shortly after the convention, to consider future strategy. Many of the women were seething with anger and pain. In one of the small discussion groups, which included Suzanne Hiatt and Carter Heyward, friends from Cambridge who had gone to Louisville, I wanted to talk about next steps, but found they were too furious to listen. Carter burst out, "Pauli, I cannot *hear* what you are saying. Strategy is not where I am at this moment. I'm trying to decide whether to leave this church."

I pleaded with her not to leave. "Do whatever you have to do, Carter," I said, "but let the church put *you* out."

The rawness of these wounds was so distressing that in the closing session I felt compelled to say that the church was losing its authority as a Christian body and that it was no longer speaking with an authentic voice if women were treated as outcasts when they sought to answer God's call to the priesthood. At that session we met jointly with a few key men who supported us, and I was struck by the contrast between each group's approach to the issue. While the women stressed the moral wrong of exclusion from ordination, the male priests were pragmatic and tough-minded, concerning themselves with ways to enlist the support of influential bishops, clergy, and strategic laypersons to ensure victory for the ordination of women at the next general convention, which would meet in Minneapolis in 1976.

I left the conference troubled because I saw no long-range plan of action directed toward the next convention. But action of a different sort was soon forthcoming. In mid-December, five male deacons were ordained to the priesthood at the Cathedral of Saint John the Divine in New York City. At the ceremony five women deacons whose qualifications were identical to those of their brethren—except for their sex—also presented themselves in vestments to Bishop Paul Moore Jr. for ordination. Women at General Seminary had been alerted that this public "witness" would take place, and several of us attended the service to give our sisters spiritual and moral support.

It was the first of several dramatic confrontations in the Episcopal Church during the next three years as the women's ordination issue rocketed into the news and almost split the church apart. When the women deacons knelt before Bishop Moore in silent appeal just before the consecration, he told them sadly, "Go in peace, my sisters." Rejected at the altar, they turned and walked with bowed heads in solemn procession down the center aisle. No funeral procession could have been more sorrowful. I was sitting in the second row just beneath the pulpit, and I raced down the side aisle to join them so they would not be alone, but when I reached the rear doors of the nave more than half of the congregation was already there. Almost everyone was crying as we held the women in our arms and let them sob on our shoulders. Then our "church in exile" went to a building nearby, where we shared in a joyous agape that had been prepared for us in place of the Holy Eucharist at the cathedral we had left behind.

The incident had immediate repercussions at General Seminary, where the community divided into warring camps. Heated exchanges took place in the corridors and in the refectory. Some male seminarians condemned the women's action as a scandal. Some who had shown lukewarm support for women's ordination now railed against using a "civil rights demonstration" tactic that, they felt, had no place in the solemn liturgy of the church. Others contented themselves with hostile stares at those of us who supported the women deacons by our presence at the ordination service. I learned that disputes among the faithful, although usually fought with polite words, can be as acrimonious in their language as a street brawl.

At times, when theological arguments were invoked against the ordination of women, I shuttled between faith and inner doubt. These arguments carried the force of a two-thousand-year tribal taboo and were so deeply embedded in the psyche that on the morning of July 29, 1974, when I took the train to Philadelphia to attend the ceremony in which eleven women deacons were ordained priests without the official approval of their own bishops, I experienced sudden terror. My panic was so great that I might have left the train at Newark if I had not met two clergywomen of the United Church of Christ, whose obvious enthusiasm for the event calmed some of my fears.

In Philadelphia, we joined a throng of two thousand people from many parts of the country, who crowded into the Church of the Advocate to witness a dramatic turning point in the struggle for women's ordination. None of us knew what to expect, although there were rumors that dissidents might try to disrupt the proceedings by seizing upon a rarely used provision in the order of service, in which the bishop says to the people, "if any of you know any impediment or crime because of which we should not proceed, come forward now, and make it known." When this point was reached in the Philadelphia ordinations, a few male priests fairly screamed their objections. Their hysterical outburst was received calmly, and when they had left the church the ceremony continued with customary beauty and solemnity. By the end of the service the joyous spirit that enveloped the congregation swept away all my doubts as to the rightness of the action taken that day. My most cherished memory of the occasion is that of kneeling before the newly priested Jeannette Piccard to receive her blessing.

This ordination was historic in more than one respect. It took place in a church in the heart of the Philadelphia ghetto, and a Negro congregation was the host. Symbolically, the rejected opened their arms to the rejected.

The Episcopal Church would never be the same after the widely publicized and much discussed "Philadelphia Ordinations." The House of Bishops called an emergency meeting and a majority of those present voted to condemn the ordinations as "invalid." Although lively debates among church scholars followed as to whether the ordinations were invalid or merely irregular, the sacramental act could not be rescinded, and the new priests could not be ignored. For many women like me, their existence revolutionized our feelings about the church and its sacraments. When a woman presided at the Holy Eucharist, we felt included in the act more completely than ever before, and were able to enter more fully into this sacred experience. In the days following Philadelphia, some of us met secretly in a small group for a house communion celebrated by one of the Eleven. When the Reverend Alison Cheek, who had been ordained in Philadelphia, became the first woman to celebrate the Holy Eucharist publicly in an Episcopal church in the United States—at Saint Stephen and the Incarnation in Washington, D.C.—my friend Morag Simchak, who attended the service, sent me an envelope containing crumbs of the consecrated bread, reverently wrapped in white paper. Public celebrations like this led to at least two canonical trials in which male rectors were charged with violating their ordination vows by permitting unauthorized persons to exercise priestly functions in their respective parish churches. These trials only fanned the flames of dissension as the church approached its next general convention.

Throughout those turbulent, unpredictable years I felt the steadying influence of seminary professors whose intellectual integrity I respected—theological scholars such as Pierson Parker, James A. Carpenter, Charles P. Price, Henry Rightor, Marianne H. Micks, and others. Their unswerving support strengthened my faith and buoyed my hope.

I had postponed my fieldwork in parish ministry until my senior year and, by getting permission from the General Seminary faculty to study at Virginia Theological Seminary that year, was able to do my field education at Saint Philip's Chapel, Aquasco, in Prince George's County, Maryland. It was the same little mission church my uncle had served as vicar in my childhood fifty years earlier. Some of the infants he had baptized then were now grandparents and leaders of the congregation, and Peter Brooks, who was the oldest communicant, remembered me as a little girl. Members of Saint Philip's had never had a seminarian serve their church before, and they were so pleased to learn that I cared enough to remember and come back to this small rural congregation that they adopted me with pride and affection. Their vicar, the Reverend William A. Jerr, took me under his wing and delighted in coaching me so that I learned to perform liturgical acts with ease.

Working at Saint Philip's was the best possible preparation for ordination. Its white wooden structure held scarcely more than a hundred people, but for me it rivaled the quality of a great cathedral. Knowing that Aunt Pauline, Aunt Sallie, and Grandmother Cornelia had all worshiped there many years before linked me with my past and gave continuity to my spiritual pilgrimage. I remained there through my graduation and ordination to the diaconate, and left only after a tragic fire destroyed the building in November 1976. The morning after the fire, I stood looking at the ruins and at the cardboard sign attached to a scarred railing, on which someone had written: "Jesus wept." I mourned the loss of that small church building as one mourns the loss of a friend. The congregation of Saint Philip's had affirmed my ministry, especially during those months of intolerable uncertainty just before the General Convention met that September in Minneapolis.

My faith had not been robust enough to hazard the possibility of still another rejection in my life, so instead of going to Minneapolis I decided to stay home and spend those fateful days in meditation and prayer. As a result, I missed the excitement when women's ordination was finally approved by the General Convention of the Episcopal Church. I was alone when I learned the result of the vote, but almost immediately afterward I got an amazing telephone call that once more linked my present and past in an almost mystical continuity. Earlier that summer I had received a letter from the Reverend Peter James Lee, rector of the Chapel of the Cross in Chapel Hill, North Carolina. The Reverend Lee wrote that he had read *Proud Shoes* [Murray's history of her family, published in 1956] and learned through it of my relationship to the nineteenth-century Smith family of Chapel Hill: how my great-grandmother, the hapless slave Harriet, who was the property of Dr. James Strudwick Smith, had been raped by young Sidney Smith and had borne a daughter, Cornelia; and how Sidney Smith's older sister, Mary Ruffin Smith, had taken her infant niece into her home and church and raised her as a devout Episcopalian. In the parish register of the Chapel of the Cross, the Reverend Lee had found the record of Grandmother Cornelia's baptism.

On the evening of the vote, Peter Lee telephoned me from Minneapolis. "I want to invite you to celebrate your first Holy Eucharist as a priest at the Chapel of the Cross," he told me. "I can think of no more appropriate symbol of what has happened here today than having you preside at the altar in the same chapel building where your Grandmother Cornelia was baptized in 1854." I was so stunned by this proposal that I stammered something unintelligible in reply, but the Reverend Lee cheerfully assured me he would write me all the details. On the same evening, my suffragan bishop from Massachusetts, the Right Reverend Morris F. Arnold, who had ordained me a deacon the previous June, called to emphasize the reality of the event. He told me that he had been thinking of me especially when the vote was being taken and now he was looking ahead to my ordination to the priesthood. He suggested that to spare the expense of my having to return to Boston for ordination in my own diocese, an arrangement could be made to have me ordained at the National Cathedral in Washington, D.C., by the Right Reverend William F. Creighton, bishop of the Diocese of Washington. I was overjoyed at this prospect. Bishop Creighton had endeared himself to women aspiring to the priesthood by announcing his refusal to ordain anyone, male or female, until the General Convention met again and passed on the women's ordination issue. The convention's approval was to become effective on January 1, 1977, and Bishop Creighton scheduled his ordination ceremony for January 8.

Although I had struggled with doubts throughout my candidacy, the greatest reassurance that I had taken the right step in applying to enter holy orders was the absence of any delay in the process leading to ordination. The timing was providential; even if I had been a man, I could not have been consecrated a priest under the most liberal application of church regulations until December 9, 1976, only a few weeks earlier than my actual ordination. During those few weeks, however, I had to meet a test of pastoral ministry for which my seminary training could not fully prepare me—ministry in the presence of death.

In early December, Adina Stewart Carrington, my friend Maida's mother, who for years had been a second mother to me and whom I called Moms, suffered a stroke, and I rushed to Brooklyn to be with her and with Maida in the crisis. My work among the sick and dying during my pastoral training at Bellevue Hospital could not shield me from the overwhelming sorrow of seeing this vibrant woman, whose home had been filled with laughter, now stricken and unable to speak to me when I entered her bedroom. She could only smile in recognition, as if to say everything was all right now that I was there. For three days Maida and I took turns watching over Moms, as her attending nurse, Maude Fleming, a devoutly religious woman, gently guided us through the subtle changes in Moms's breathing and pulse rate, which signaled her approaching death. When the end came, all three of us were sitting by her bedside reading from the Bible, and as Maida read the Ninety-first Psalm aloud, her mother gave a slight gasp and slipped into eternity.

Mrs. Fleming sent Maida out of the room and pressed me into service to assist her with post-death ministrations, performed with tenderness as if Moms were still alive and could respond to us. Maida had been determined that her mother would die with dignity in the familiar surroundings of her own home. She had succeeded. In death, all pain had vanished from her mother's face, and although she was a woman of eighty, she looked like a beautiful young girl who had fallen asleep. My final test came when I took part in Moms's funeral as a member of the clergy and read the Ninety-first Psalm without letting my voice falter.

Beginning January 1, 1977, the first ordinations of women as Episcopal priests became media events. As each ceremony took place, it was headlined in the news as "the first woman priest in the United States," or "the first woman priest in New York State," or in Virginia or in California. On Saturday, January 8, I was one of three women and three men to be ordained at the same service in which the ordination of two "irregular" women priests was affirmed, all at the Washington cathedral. The circumstances gave the ceremony unusual prominence.

Several days before the ordination, I was suddenly seized by an agony of indecision, as though I had been assaulted by an army of demons. The thought that the opponents of women's ordination might be right and that I might be participating in a monstrous wrong terrified me. As a sister priest put it later, speaking of herself, "I felt that God might strike me dead before it happened." I have since been told by other priests, male and female, that they faced a similar ordeal just before their ordination, but at the time I thought this ambivalence was peculiar to me, so personal that I dared not speak to anyone about it. I prayed fervently for some sign that I was doing God's will.

January 8 was a bitter-cold, gray morning in Washington, with ice and snow covering the ground, but three thousand or more people packed the Washington National Cathedral, a number of them my relatives and close friends. As was customary, a long procession of vested clergy walked down the aisle, followed by the lay presenters (or sponsors) of the ordinands. Then those of us who were being ordained proceeded to our individual prayer desks, which were arranged in a semicircle around the Great Transept, and the participating clergy and elaborately robed bishops continued up into the chancel. The familiar liturgy moved forward majestically through the presentation, declaration of vows, litany for ordination, sermon, examination, and consecration. I was the last of the six to be consecrated, and was told later that just as Bishop Creighton placed his hands upon my forehead, the sun broke through the clouds outside and sent shafts of rainbow-colored light down through the stained-glass windows. The shimmering beams of light were so striking that members of the congregation gasped. When I learned about it later, I took it as the sign of God's will I had prayed for. Immediately after we were consecrated and vested in our white chasubles, and the words "The Peace of the Lord be always with you" had been spoken, the cathedral throng exploded in a joyous outburst such as one seldom sees at a staid Episcopal service. It was a resounding affirmation of our call to serve God as priests.

Five weeks later, on the weekend of Abraham Lincoln's birthday, I traveled to North Carolina to celebrate my first Holy Eucharist—also the first Eucharist to be celebrated by a woman in that state—at the Chapel of the Cross in Chapel Hill. Family history and religious tradition combined with changing folkways to make it an occasion of high drama, which attracted not only the local media but also Charles Kuralt of CBS—himself a graduate of the University of North Carolina—who came down with his *On the Road* van and television crew from New York to cover the event.

On Sunday, February 13, in the little chapel where my Grandmother Cornelia had been baptized more than a century earlier as one of "Five Servant Children Belonging to Miss Mary Ruffin Smith," I read the gospel from an ornate lectern engraved with the name of that slave-owning woman who had left part of her wealth to the Episcopal Diocese of North Carolina. A thoroughly interracial congregation crowded the chapel, and many more stood outside until they could enter to kneel at the altar rail and receive Communion. There was great irony in the fact that the first woman priest to preside at the altar of the church to which Mary Ruffin Smith had given her deepest devotion should be the granddaughter of the little girl she had sent to the balcony reserved for slaves. But more than irony marked that moment. Whatever future ministry I might have as a priest, it was given to me that day to be a symbol of healing.

All the strands of my life had come together. Descendant of slave and of slave owner, I had already been called poet, lawyer, teacher, and friend. Now I was empowered to minister the sacrament of One in whom there is no north or south, no black or white, no male or female—only the spirit of love and reconciliation drawing us all toward the goal of human wholeness.

When Woods Are Dark

The Enchantment of the Infinite

SENA JETER NASLUND

1.

In the beginning, language was my conduit to the spiritual—no doubt—but also the senses, particularly the senses of hearing and sight, and also something like the sense of touch but touch expanded by imagination: the spatial sense. My earliest memory of a spiritual moment was through that potent combination of language and sound we call song, and I remember acutely the time and place of vivid singing, perhaps because that moment had the novelty of introducing a congeries of ideas, in addition to being a spiritual experience.

Four years old, I was in Sunday school at Norwood Methodist Church, in my home neighborhood of Norwood just off the northern edge of Birmingham, Alabama, when my mother, a very fine musician who played piano for the Sunday school because I was a member of the class, nodded affirmatively after a teacher's unexpected announcement that now Sena would stand and sing "A Little Star" all by herself. I stood. My mother was already seated at the piano, with hands hovering over the keys; she played a small introductory musical phrase, then nodded slightly at me, and I began to sing:

A little star creeps over the hill
When woods are dark and birds are still
The children fold their hands in prayer,
And the Love of God is everywhere.

A meditative song, lento, in a minor key. But how did anyone know that I knew the song? My voice was not particularly pleasing (I had trouble singing high notes), but I was not afraid, though this request was *unfamiliar*. While I didn't know how it would turn out, I would simply try and thus find out what it meant to stand and perform. Surprisingly, as I began to sing I was given a new voice, one high, pure, and sweet, a remarkable voice, but one that I knew might be there for this one and only occasion. It seemed each moment must have its own unique nature, but now, in this moment, I realized the leadership was up to me because Mama was *accompanying* my singing with utmost attention, though she could play circles around me, Bach, Beethoven, Brahms, Chopin, Debussy, and "Sabre Dance" and "Flight of the Bumblebee." And I realized that as I sang, all those words written in the present tense were coming true: that I could see a star creeping over a hill while I stood before dark woods, and I could imagine little birds sitting still on branches in the interiors of trees, and, yes, beyond the natural scene of star, hill, and woods, I could imagine children, all over the world at dusk, inside houses kneeling by their beds with hands pressed together even though I was a child in another moment *not* praying before bedtime when woods are dark but standing up Sunday morning in a room with other children, and that over it all, like my mother's hands over the world of the keyboard, was love, invisible but present, hovering in the space over woods and houses, and love was much the same as God (not a person after all, but a feeling), and that there was a concept called "everywhere," a place of infinite expansion that, yes, I could imagine.

With one eye on the actual world and one on what was envisioned, two different moments could be experienced simultaneously. As the transparency of complex thought became apparent, I existed in a way I had not existed before I sang. Often in childhood, particularly when walking by myself along the grassy Norwood Boulevard while thinking hard, I said to myself: "Remember this, when you grow up, that when you were still little you could understand *everything, EVERYTHING.*" (Nonetheless, I must admit that a voice in my head now sometimes compulsively queries of myself, "What do you really know about *anything?*")

A Sunday school song I disliked was "Jesus Loves Me." My dislike was rooted in a misunderstanding of language; I heard the phrase "this I know" as "this sino," and I was puzzled as to what a "sino" was but decided it must be related to a silo; thus, Jesus emerged from the line "Jesus loves me, this sino" as a tall granary, but why were there no images of pigs and chickens if this was a song about a farm? The sino seemed stuck in, aesthetically, not related to the rest of the song. I also disliked the explanation "'cause the Bible tells me so" which smacked of a kind of adult logic that melted down to "because I say so." The tone of the song seemed smugly self-centered to me, not expansive at all. And I was *not* weak, as the song stated.

On the other hand, there was a picture in the spacious Sunday school room of a kindly, seated Jesus, in a white robe with a shepherd's staff, surrounded by children of various colors and ethnicities leaning against his knees and shoulders, and this picture helped a great deal in the visualization of another song, whose ideas I liked:

Jesus loves the little children
All the children of the world
Red and yellow, black and white
They are precious in his sight.
Jesus loves the little children of the world.

In their last lines, both of the two songs that appealed to my imagination engage in a rhetoric of expansion—*everywhere* in "A Little Star," the broad and variously populated *world* in the second song—and both songs are variations on a theme of "love" as embodied first in peaceful nature and, in the second case, in the human figure of Jesus, the one annexed for the sake of the song from the picture on the wall.

Years later, I quoted those lines of the preciousness of "red and yellow, black and white," as the epigraph to my novel *Four Spirits* about the civil rights movement in Birmingham. The book is dedicated to the four girls killed in 1963 in the racist, terrorist bombing of Sixteenth Street Baptist Church. While "A Little Star" found its climactic expression, for me, in *Ahab's Wife,* subtitled *The Star-Gazer,* a book with a rather Wordsworthian pantheism, *Four Spirits* addresses the side of spirituality manifest in social activism and a commitment to racial equality.

As a child, notions of spiritual realities moved in and out of my body as naturally as the air I breathed when I sang. Those intimations of the spiritual were part of me and part of the medium in which I had my being. And I held them dear, initially, because they were *beautiful.* When I was almost five, more pragmatic questions arose about what happens after death and about the relation of daily behavior to the afterlife.

My grandmother Sena Sewanee Carter Jeter, who lived next door across the red clay driveway, was very ill, and apparently older children knew she might die. As we stood beside the open garage door at the head of the driveway, the older children discussed Grandma's fate. The left-hand door was swung wide open, and children stood on both sides of it—boys, I remember, probably my two older brothers and maybe Don who lived on the other side of us, or Mike Brooks. While they talked, I contemplated an open knothole in the wood of the door. I touched it repeatedly and laced my fingers from one side of the planks, through the knothole, to the other side. It was a fascinating hole, irregular in shape, with smooth thick edges. Someone—perhaps Mike or Don, because I had not heard the idea before—remarked that grandmother was a good person and would go to heaven. It was an astonishing concept: that there was a heaven after death, that goodness in life got you there. The idea was reassuring. By the judgment and decree of a jury of children, it seemed the matter was settled: my grandmother bearing my own first name would go to heaven. I need not worry.

When my grandmother did die, I had the chicken pox and was quite ill, but I remember my doctor father carrying me over to touch her as she lay in her coffin. In her hand she held a pale pink rose cut from the bushes beside the house where she had lived with Aunt Kumi and Aunt Pet. My father told me to touch her, and I did, on the forehead, with one finger as I, covered with chicken pox, leaned out of his arms. Perhaps he said that now I would never be afraid of death, or perhaps he had expressed that idea earlier, when he gathered me up in his arms to cross the driveway. Or I may have only imagined such an explanation for a child's being asked to touch the dead. I'm sure that my father wanted me to remember his mother and her passing, and that the sense of touch was one of his allies in causing memory to take root. Certainly my touching of the knothole in the garage door had had something to do with a nascent metaphysical awareness of the two-sidedness of the reality of that door, though only one side was visible at any given moment.

By the age of six, the known world had become larger, with

quite a number of things in it. I knew that various people over history had had different gods because I knew Bubba and John, my brothers, read about the Greek gods and goddesses in the *Iliad,* and that Zeus, the most powerful and fatherlike, was something like the one we called God, who had angels rather than lesser gods for company.

Throughout this early childhood, I knew that I myself was exceptionally fleet of foot (like a junior goddess), strong, a good wrestler, unafraid of racing or fighting with anyone reasonably near my size. And I did fight, having a strong urge to assert my will onto other people and the world around me. I also sometimes pilfered small items from friends, so strong was the urge to gather the goodies of the world to myself, as part of my own definition, not theirs. I knew this was not good behavior. And my conscience smote me terrifically, especially since I also sometimes lost my temper, bore grudges, and told lies to get out of such "trouble."

I felt very guilty. Up to age eight, I devised little punishments for myself, not in response to any particular misdeed, but in answer to a generalized sense of guilt. For example, I would make myself fold into a cardboard box and stay there or make myself march round and round in the hot sun. Perhaps I also pursued intensity, or extremity, for its own sake. Nonetheless, these humiliations of the flesh seemed in themselves shameful to me, and I told no one about them and took care that no one saw what I was doing. I feel somewhat uncomfortable telling about these deeds now. Eventually, about age eight, I resolved not to enact these punishments anymore since they themselves made me feel more guilty and somehow *nasty.*

Since age six, I had felt curious about the consequences of bad and good deeds—not so much in terms of parental punishment or heavenly reward but in terms of the observable universe. I hypothesized that there was a *moral order,* something like the *law of grav-*

ity, to the universe, though I didn't have the phrase *moral order*
then. (In my short story "How Do You Do, Mister Cat?" a fictive
character wonders the same thing as a child.) I decided to test the
idea, though I cannot remember where I picked up the possibility
of experimentation.

Ah, I do remember: I used to want to fly, very much, and I often
had flying dreams as a young child, as I still do. Because the dreams
seemed so convincingly real and my knowledge of practical physics
was certainly incomplete, I decided to try the dream methods of
flying the next morning. If in a dream I could fly by pedaling fast,
as I did on my tricycle, I tried out that method in morning sun-
shine, leaping off a bank while pedaling furiously. *That* was how
I came to understand the concept of experimentation.

(And there were other early tests of reality that took place before I went to school at age six: one was spying on the little cowboy
figures I played with on the rug to see if they conducted lives of
their own, beyond my controlling, when they thought I wasn't
watching. I hoped they did. As a fiction writer, I do love it, even
now, when my characters suddenly do something beyond my plan-
ning or controlling.)

For the question of the moral order of the universe, I devised
a number system for both good and bad deeds—the higher the
number, the more extreme the deed—according to my intuition
about their heft, along with a corresponding number system for
rewards and punishments. With this conceptual apparatus, I kept
a running tally to see if, without human agency, I was rewarded
appropriately for the good and punished "accidentally" but appropriately for the bad that I did. Perhaps the idea originated in my
mother's laughingly referring to a Gilbert and Sullivan line, "Let
the punishment fit the crime." When I was cross with a friend,
soon after, but in an entirely different context, I found that I might
suffer a seemingly undeserved disapproving look from my Aunt

Kumi. When I was generous to another child, the universe sent me an unearned kindness with an equal degree of intensity. My moral calculus revealed to me that there was indeed a moral order! A moral order did not reside with mere human figures of authority but hovered *everywhere*. While this idea helped me a great deal to control my impulses to fight, to lie, to seek revenge, to steal, it subverted the earlier sense of the infinitude of everywhere as a more purely spiritual reality. I became better behaved, but morality and behavior became more significant to me than spirituality and the inner life for a while.

In fact, so far as I was concerned, the inner life had often seemed represented by various emotional states. One day as I sat on the back steps—age four?—I had watched my father drive away, down that long clay driveway to go to work in West Virginia as the doctor for a coal mining company, and I recognized that I felt peculiar: *sad,* the word came to me out of nowhere. And then I thought, *This is what they mean by sad.* For the first time I matched up a nebulous feeling with a specific word, and words became much more interesting to me. A fictional version of this scene occurs in my novel *Ahab's Wife* when Una, as a child, discovers the language to describe how she felt when her father drove away, in a buggy.

When I was grown, my mother told a similar story of herself as a very young child of age two or three: she was lying in her backyard in McFall, Missouri, looking at the clouds when she thought, *Beautiful. So that is what they mean by beautiful.* (Are our spirits gene-dependent in their makeup? Whatever the cause, it pleases me and connects me to my mother that the same English phrase "that is what they mean" would occur to both of us, at an extremely young age, for the sake of linking language to the inner life.)

After the discovery of the moral order, I sometimes felt depression —I don't know why. The idea of *order* was a reassuring one. Besides guilt at my misdeeds, at ages six, seven, and eight, I also felt not just sad, as I had when my father drove away, but a generalized depression during the holidays leading up to Christmases those three years. I felt there was something wrong with me, that I did not experience what people called *the Christmas spirit,* though I loved singing Christmas carols around the piano with my brothers and hearing my mother ritualistically read aloud "'Twas the Night Before Christmas" on Christmas Eve; I was always quite pleased with my toys and gifts, which were not particularly numerous but were always exactly what I'd hoped for. And I liked the biblical Christmas story, and the Christmas pageant at Norwood Methodist Church. Still, there seemed to be something wrong with my spirit or my essence, though I tried hard to appear to be what I referred to as "normal." Perhaps I felt depression because I knew that even good behavior and acceptable appearances did not substitute for an inner spiritual identity.

Throughout those same years of six through eight, my awareness of my moral imperfections—particularly my sins of commission against other children—troubled me enough that I often had insomnia, despite knowing also that I was smart, successful in school, strong and quick in neighborhood play, and that I had a best friend of extremely satisfying congeniality in Nancy, who lived close by and who liked to "pretend" as much as I did. I filled the wakeful, guilty hours by imagining stories so that I could lie still in bed, as though I were asleep; then no one would guess I was such a bad child that I could not sleep at night. I had no central core, no identity, or spirit, that transcended the problems of mundane behavior, and I felt eroded by all my shortcomings.

2.

Everything changed at age nine. Some neighborhood child invited me to a once-a-week Bible class, held in the gray basement of a

neighbor woman, a fundamentalist Christian. Mrs. G. told us boys
and girls that we were indeed all sinners—it was rather a relief to
hear an adult say what I already knew in my heart—and that there
was a perfect and complete remedy: we had but to believe that Jesus
was the Son of God and ask forgiveness of our sins; then we would
be forgiven, the Holy Spirit would come to dwell in our hearts, and
when we died we would go to heaven. She carefully explained that
it was not living a good life that provided access to heaven, though
we should obey the Ten Commandments and do good; no, simple
belief, even if espoused only at the very last minute before death,
was the ticket. I embraced the ideas as fast as I could. Guilt lifted
from me, and in its place came devotion to serving God. My faith
was that whatever I had done was forgiven; whatever I might do
could be forgiven. I began my own serious reading of the Bible.

I continued attending the Methodist church, but I became increasingly dissatisfied with the lack of emphasis on fundamental
belief. The Methodists seemed lax about behavior, too. Mrs. G.
told us it was wrong to play cards, to drink, to smoke, to dance,
even to go to the movies (which might awaken improper feelings).
She was a kindly person, but embracing these strictures cut me off
from two important pleasures of my peers—movies and dancing.
One of my friends even found a biblical directive about not braid-
ing one's hair, and I tried to stop doing that though I was now playing the cello and unbraided hair could easily get ensnared in the
strings and pegs close to my cheek. I thought seriously about becoming a Christian missionary to Africa, as both of Mrs. G's older
children were in the process of doing.

To be relieved of guilt and to be able to pray to a loving and
forgiving God more than made up for any trivial social depriva-
tions, and a ponytail helped keep my hair out of the cello strings.
Nonetheless, life did not become simple: oddly, I didn't want my
parents to know how devout I had become. They were themselves

quite liberal, and I felt ashamed of my obsession with nightly Bible reading. Often I waited till everyone else had gone to bed to read the Bible. I prayed in the bathroom, behind the one door in the house that had a lock to insure privacy. I remember yet the cold, hard hexagonal tiles on my bare knees, the cool, smooth edge of the tub, which I used rather like an altar rail. But there, with God, I felt free to review all my troubles, which were now less centered on behavior and more on an imperfect emotional life. Through prayer I learned to gain access in an honest way to my own anxieties, hopes, fears. I could ask for specific help about my temper, about the inability to forgive, about jealousy of others. And, miraculously, I could see such character flaws melt away: prayer alleviated these unwanted emotions which I considered ignoble. Being honest about my feelings and thoughts, with trust that all was forgiven, helped me to know myself, to be comfortable, to change for the better, and to espouse values that are still of central importance to me.

When I was fifteen, though he never smoked, my father died of lung cancer. While I was a devout Christian (despite my efforts to be unobtrusive in my devotions, my father knew and accepted that I was religious, giving me a large-print Bible one Christmas so that I wouldn't hurt my eyes reading small print and enclosing a notecard supporting my sense of myself as Christian), the traditional images of heaven as the place where my father had gone offered me less than solace. They didn't seem real. I did not recuse God: people died—a fact of life. The imperative to my mind was to imagine nonbeing. I felt I had to know what it would be like to imagine one's own nonexistence. My mind worked on the problem constantly. I knew nonbeing logically had no attributes, so how could I imagine it?

The reader will have to take on faith that one gray spring day (my father had been buried at Helicon on Thanksgiving Day, his favorite holiday) I did imagine nonbeing. One late afternoon, I was waiting for the bus to pick me up on Seventh Avenue to ride home to Norwood from Phillips High School, when I realized, "I've got it. There it is." (I am sorry—there's no content to be described.) But I knew I had gone to that place of nonbeing *in my imagination,* that I would never forget it, and that I could will myself to go there at any time when I needed to confront that reality. (Why would I need to go there? For honesty's sake.) For years afterward, I would occasionally practice, to see if I could still imagine nonbeing, and I could. (For perhaps the last two decades—I wonder if it's been since the birth of Flora, my daughter—I've had no call to go there. Instead, when I need to journey, I set to imagining the realms of my novels.)

That I could imagine nonbeing seemed to affect my Christian belief in no way. At sixteen I did decide to become a medical missionary and got baptized at Norwood Methodist Church. Mrs. G. had moved from Norwood, but she invited me and two of my dear friends, Janice and Juanita, also her disciples, over to spend the night one time, and I continued to feel connected to her and, for several years, to the fundamentalist Christian beliefs she had shared at a time when I much needed them.

In recounting this period of intense Christianity, ages nine to nineteen, I need to linger over the idea that I was sustained in my Christian belief by my friendship with Janice L. and her sister Juanita. More than being saved, having Janice for a neighborhood friend and later as a classmate gave me great daily happiness. During grades four through eight, after Nancy moved away, I usually felt like an outsider at school, despite knowing gifted Joan Morris and forming a close bond with the amazing newcomer Wanda LaRue during grades seven and eight. Though we were not in the same classes, Janice and Juanita lived nearby; because of their friendship, I was not alone. To stand with Janice and sing

"What a Friend We Have in Jesus" meant much was right with the world and with my soul: I also had a beloved friend right there.

Instead of "pretending" and acting out our own stories as I had with Nancy, Janice and I read many of the same books and talked about our favorite parts; sometimes with Juanita and Wanda, we tape-recorded radio-play versions of the texts, with background music and sound effects. Juanita and I often dissolved in delicious giggles when either of us tried to speak in a deep male voice. At Phillips High School, Janice and I often sat in the same classrooms, admired the same teachers, shared other studious friends, went to Norwood Methodist together (including a fabulous trip to Lake Junaluska); we both loved classical music, practiced piano or cello, worked to become good public speakers, studied our brains out, sewed dresses together, and held the same values. We spent many a summer day and weekend, Janice, Juanita, and I, lying on a bedspread in their yard under the Chinese elm tree, playing board games, or badminton, or croquet, or walking stilts, strolling, riding our bicycles, roller skating, swinging, or climbing trees "down by the railroad track" where we sat and talked endlessly. Our leisure time together was a kind of heaven all its own, the counterbalance to the seriousness with which we took school.

During this rather idyllic time in high school where friendship, faith, and scholarship intermingled, I had an example of sterling goodness in a male figure in our youth director at church—Ben Price—who was a college student at Birmingham-Southern. Admired and loved by all the high-school people under his guidance, Ben played the piano with fluency and intended to become a medical missionary, though eventually Ben, now deceased, became a pediatrician in Birmingham. I still cherish his gentle kindness and inclusiveness.

It surprised me when Janice, too, decided not to become a medical missionary, but said she really liked working math problems and perhaps would go on from high school to study math. I was more extreme: to me, if one was a Christian, then saving others was of paramount importance. But I knew, intuitively, that there was something unhealthy, or unrealistic, about my extremism and that Janice had a sense of balance I lacked. She was more reasonable, though she too had refrained from movies and dancing.

My even longer-term friend Nancy provided another check to my fanaticism. Since I was three years old, I had reveled in my friendship with Nancy, who moved away when we were about eight. Nancy and I still talked on the telephone and visited each other from time to time; we, too, had an immense amount of fun together. But somehow I didn't want to bother Nancy with my intense belief system. She seemed too sensible for such fanaticism. With Nancy, as we grew into our teens, we could talk about our bodies, boys, breasts, even sex.

3.

When I went to Birmingham-Southern College, I found what it was that I really loved to do with my mind. Janice had already discovered her love of math; I discovered that I loved to read and analyze poetry: *How Does a Poem Mean?* (a textbook by John Ciardi) was the bible directing my new thought pattern. Suddenly this approach to literature, as taught by Dr. Cecil Abernethy, dean of the college, seemed more liberating than any approach to life. It actually seemed possible to understand thoroughly how a short poem worked. Up until this time, I felt I could understand whatever my teachers explained to me; now I felt that I could analyze for myself how language conveyed meaning, especially when it was packaged not as divine writ but as human creations, as poems. Soon the same methods of "close reading" could be applied to prose fiction as well. The abstractions of philosophical discourse became so many balls to juggle in the air, and *what* the philosophers meant could be understood as well. New, close friends emerged, people I hadn't known throughout childhood and high school, but people who had a cast of mind (all on their own) that resonated with my new interests.

Despite my joy in these new mental powers, I had a very difficult time justifying a change in vocation, from premed (so I could be a medical missionary) to the study of literature. I felt I must "do good" in the world, and the world of reading was the only one that gave me great pleasure. I talked about this dilemma with new friends. Almost all of them felt we had a right to pursue what we enjoyed studying; our natural talents, to them, took justifiable precedence over any idea of moral imperative, just as Janice had felt in high school. To some extent my spiritual devotion had come to stand between me and my natural self.

That in mature adulthood I eventually recovered my early childhood joy in my selfhood was clear to me one day when my present husband, John, and I were courting. One evening we were sitting on the brick patio behind my little house, enjoying the end of day and the gathering of bats chasing insects in the dusk, when he proposed that we might travel together to Third World countries to be witnesses and possibly help with the hardships and dangers to be found in such places. I said no, that I didn't want to. Somewhat heatedly, he replied, "All you really want to do is stay in your house and write." I jumped from my chair, stamped my foot, and said vehemently, "Yes! That *is* what I want to do. That's what I *am* doing, and that's what I'm *going* to do!" Not long after that declaration, I found the courage to approach a novel of greater scope than I'd ever dreamed of before—a huge project, *Ahab's Wife*.

But it was many years before I was able to claim my birthright. Not only the study of literature but also the study of philosophy at Birmingham-Southern was an important step toward the

future. First I was taken with the Christian existentialists, especially Paul Tillich and his book *The Courage to Be,* and eventually the atheistic existentialists. I found that Sartre's mind, in *Being
and Nothingness,* had gone places similar to my own effort, at fifteen when my father died, to imagine nonexistence; that Camus
had a stark honesty that was very attractive, if frightening; that
Herman Hesse wrote about people who were seekers, who enter-
tained mystical ideas beyond Christianity. The so-called Problem
of Evil seemed beyond solving, to my mind, in Judeo-Christian
terms: given human suffering, how can God be omniscient, om-
nipotent, and good? I studied the book of Job in a liberal setting
and did not find God's behavior acceptable. In short, my fundamentalist Christian beliefs began to loosen their grip on my mind,
spirit, and body. My evolution was like shedding an old skin, just
as natural and painless.

In this philosophical adventure, I had a new friend, another
Janice, who was just as taken with philosophy and its relevance to
the kind of existence we chose for ourselves as the first Janice had
been with Christianity. I was not lonely in my new belief system.
While we questioned ideas about God, we felt no immediate need
to dismiss him. In the context of the overwhelming racial injustice
of the South and the Birmingham civil rights movement of the six-
ties, belief in God and in Christianity was an extremely positive
source of strength and courage. The unjust position of women in
American society also began to emerge, sometimes in ironic contrast to the way Christianity was practiced in some of the white,
male-dominated churches. Janice E. was denied a permanent position at a Baptist church as a choir director solely and frankly
because she was female. To question, to think rigorously, to be
honest in introspection, to examine assumptions—all these giddy
activities gave much pleasure, but they were grafted onto an ethic
founded on basic, rather than fundamentalist, Christianity.

Part of what I chastely loved about David, my first college boyfriend, was his spiritual nature; he was kind, musically talented with a liberal eye for art and poetry, a leader in his Methodist church, and an inspiring church organist. He revered not dogma, but artistic expression as an aspect of engagement with the spiritual.

As I realized my own power to think fearlessly and unfettered by convention, I began to have a sense of myself that transcended questions of daily behavior. Nonetheless, during this time I sometimes felt like a social failure; I could not will myself to conquer shyness, but now, for relief, I turned not to the language of prayer but to writing in a notebook "dedicated to myself and the preservation of sanity." *Scriptotherapy* is the term my friend and colleague at the University of Louisville has given me. Depression came when I felt my failure to connect to clearly congenial friends; the remedy had two parts: (1) to write honestly for myself about my inadequacies, and (2) to forgive myself. If depression interfered not with my sleep but with my ability to focus on my studies, then I took out my ever-present notebook and wrote till my soul was easy. To study, to learn, was the major goal. And gradually the desire became more fine-tuned: to learn to write the kind of literature that so delighted me to read. I was able to turn to literature from premed chemistry (which I failed three times), when my friend Dwight pointed out to me, most convincingly by speaking of his own case, that literature offered invaluable psychological insights and did, in fact, "do good."

In a literature class, Dr. Cecil Abernethy posed the question, "How are Huck Finn and Pip of Dickens's *Great Expectations* alike?" Neither I nor anyone else in the class knew the answer, but I knew intuitively that the answer was of utmost importance to Dwight, sitting across the aisle. I held my breath, waiting for the answer. Dr. Abernethy said, "They're both young men in search of a father"; I knew that the statement gave illuminating focus to Dwight for his own confusion. As we left the classroom, we just looked at each other, and he asked, "How can you doubt that literature can do much good?" I answered, "Yes. I know." It was a moment of epiphany for me.

During my time at Birmingham-Southern, one of my kind professors, Leon Driskell, decided it would do me good to go beyond Alabama to Vermont, to the Bread Loaf Writers' Conference, which was directed by John Ciardi, author of the liberating textbook on poetry I had studied. Though I had no money for such an adventure, Leon Driskell raised the necessary funds. The first night at Bread Loaf, I came out of my cabin and beheld the clear night sky swarming with stars. Because of the smog from the Birmingham steel mills, I had never seen such celestial splendor. I ran back into the cabin calling, "Come quick! There's been a cosmic explosion!" I was afraid and full of wonder. The other young people came outside, then said nonchalantly, "It's like that every night." I found this idea hard to believe, but looking at the night sky, I felt like a new-hatched duckling imprinting on its mother for the first time.

4.

Decades later, celebrating the publication of my third book, *Sherlock in Love*, I felt the echo of that Bread Loaf experience of the starry starry sky. One bright day in the fall of 1993, I was in Boston, driving a small rented car, feeling inordinately on top of the world: there had been dinner parties and book signings; NPR had just given a stunningly favorable review of the book; I was in a strange and large city driving an unfamiliar car, and I was not lost. Suddenly I had a vision and heard a voice. The vision was of a woman on a roof walk, or widow's walk; it was night and she was looking out to sea, hoping to see her husband's whaling ship coming home. As she looked at the dark waves, she realized he was not coming home, not that night, not ever. With that realization, her gaze shifted from the dark water to the black sky, filled with stars. Contemplating the starry sky, she began to ask, "Who am I, in the face of all this vast glory? What's my place in the universe?" No longer was she waiting for her husband to come home and define her as wife, or in any other way; instead she was beginning to ask her own spiritual questions and to seek her own answers. Then the voice said, "Captain Ahab was neither my first husband nor my last," and with that I knew I had the concept of a new book, to be titled somewhat ironically *Ahab's Wife.*

Between the undergraduate days of Bread Loaf and envisioning *Ahab's Wife,* I had been through two marriages, each of them happy (and unhappy) in their own ways. With Michael Callaghan, classical music had become the living metaphor for the spiritual life. What could expand the soul was the beauty of music. Michael also shared his brilliant love of philosophy and German literature with me. During those days in graduate school at the University of Iowa, I studied Virginia Woolf for the first time, and my values became consonant with the credo of Bloomsbury: I pledged allegiance to personal relationships and to the truth of art—written, visual, musical.

Alan Naslund, like my first writing teacher at Birmingham-Southern, Richebourg Gaillard McWilliams, quoted Sir Philip Sydney to me, from *Astrophel and Stella:* " 'Fool,' said my Muse to me, 'look in thy heart, and write.' " On the birth of our beloved daughter, Flora, I tried harder to follow Sydney's advice about subject matter and tone. I knew that I must go deeper in my writing than I ever had before, that I must choose to write about what had been of sustaining value to me in difficult times, that I needed to affirm the preciousness of life. Alan's own talent as a writer both enthralled me and enlarged my understanding, particularly of the lens that metaphor can provide.

5.

In my most recent novel, *Four Spirits,* I have tried to honor the time of traditional Christian faith in my own life: how, in the civil rights movement of the 1960s South—led by such ministers as Martin Luther King Jr. and the Reverend Fred Shuttlesworth—for a shining moment in history, nonviolence had the victory over violence as a means of achieving greater social justice and racial equality, and love and forgiveness triumphed over hatred and retaliation. And I tell the story of how a confused college student, Stella Silver, the daughter of a doctor and a musical mother, began to sort out her own religious questions, her obligations to activism, her sense of friendship, of finding an appropriate mate, of the promise of life itself. With *Four Spirits* I wrote the novel—aided and abetted by family and friends, my agent and editor—I had promised myself to attempt forty years before, standing on the streets of Birmingham while the world changed, charging myself to *remember, remember.*

But let me back up, to the writing of the novel before *Four Spirits.* After my second marriage ended, I took up the habit of bedtime reading again, but now, in place of reading the Bible or philosophy, I found that what I wanted to read was physics and astronomy. By reading about the infinitesimal and of the magnitude and nature of the infinite cosmos, I felt an expansiveness that seemed of a spiritual nature to me. The vastness of the universe and the movement of the mind toward it offered a kind of glory. Was the brain, as Emily Dickinson suggested, bigger than the sky? Or as big? Or simply irradiated and redeemed in the act of wonder? Was this a secular version of the answer cum question given Job: "Where were you when I made the morning stars to sing together?" Instead of trying to imagine nothingness, now the imaginative task was to try to approach the enormity of the universe.

Two years of such nighttime reading stood behind the Boston experience and the voice and vision that engendered the concept of *Ahab's Wife; or, the Star-Gazer.*

With the emotional support of John Morrison and dear friends, I resolved to write precisely the book that was in my heart to write. I didn't always know what I was doing. At one point, visiting my friend and former student the novelist Lucinda Sullivan, I read a collection of extracts from poems that she had transcribed in gold handwriting onto a white tablecloth in a room housing her telescope. All the quoted lines were about the stars. Here is the quotation from a poem by one of my former students, our friend the poet Maureen Morehead:

One must take off her fear, like clothing.
One must travel at night.
This is the seeking after God.

Upon reading Maureen's lines, my half-written novel clicked into focus. Those lines, the book's epigraph, became the compass for my writing of *Ahab's Wife:* that a naked honesty is required, and courage; that each of us must face the darkness without and within; that movement and expansion are essential; that the seeking for our own spiritual life, in our own way, is our right and our necessity for authenticity. I knew the novel would be the story of a spiritual quest in the context of various friendships; I knew the book would honor the effort to respond to personal pain, to loss, and to human limitations not through destructiveness, as Melville's Ahab had, but through creativity, the making of something new; I knew this narrative would be about coming to feel at one with the universe.

Near the end of the novel, as they stand on a Nantucket roof walk to look not at a single star creeping over a hill but at the glittery array of the starry sky, Una's lover asks: "And what do you think of these heartless immensities?" Una responds, "That we are a part of them and they are a part of us."

Sex, Race, and the Stained-Glass Window

SYLVIA RHUE

The race card—since Rodney King and OJ, we have heard this buzz phrase a lot. Handy as it may be for journalists, it hides the complex interactions between viewer and viewed, black and white, male and female. In fact, as anyone who has grown up in an African American community knows, the race card is inseparable from the gender card or even, surprisingly enough, the God card. Therapists—often the soft police of the dominant culture—are also guilty of reinforcing one-dimensional notions of race. Perhaps a personal story will counter some of the simplistic thinking, a story about how it feels to come of age and come out in a Christian fundamentalist African American community.

Genesis

I grew up in a traditional African American church, which is to say that both the choir director and the organist were gay. The closet was full, and people of all sexual orientations winked and hoodwinked their way around the sexual terror that was produced by fundamentalist doctrine.

The "don't ask, don't tell" policy demanded by compulsory heterosexuality was strictly enforced and constantly policed. It was as overbearing as a drill sergeant in full regalia, marching up and down the aisles to check if everyone was still straight. When he looked us in the eye we'd sit up and salute, "No fags here, sir," "No dykes here, sir!" On he marched. Those caught or found out were asked to repent, or die.

My church was also traditional because it was racially segregated. Eleven a.m. Sunday has always been the most visible hour of apartheid in America. In churches like mine that believe in the Saturday Sabbath, the same holds true for 11 a.m. Saturday.

I mention race because the arbiters of sexual behavior in our church were white men who ruled from afar, and because James Baldwin was right when he said, in an interview published in *James Baldwin: The Legacy,* "The sexual question and the racial question have always been intertwined."

Those strange and distant white men owned the religion, the doctrine, and the tithes. They didn't call us "nigger" to our faces, since "heathen" and "pickaninny" seemed to suffice. Calling us "you people" was downright progressive. In their theological universe, a church separated by race is only logical, since heaven itself is segregated. Nothing personal. Just being logical.

Those strange and distant white men sent out written directives on correct Christian behavior: "Single people who are dating should wait six months before embarking on the first kiss." Dancing was forbidden in order to keep the naughty parts from touching. Makeup and jewelry were verboten because women were to be modest and circumspect. According to the worldview of those lofty white men, lust was lurking everywhere.

Even married parishioners had to keep their genital activity in strict compliance with the directives. For married couples: "The mouth should not go below the navel." A mouth that wandered below the navel could only be a bad mouth, doing bad things.

"You should not listen to music that causes the foot to tap." Such music was considered seductive. It could lead to lewd and lascivious behavior. It could lead to making you feel like you were a real, live, living human being. And where could that kind of thing lead to? It was all so logical.

There was a kind of reptilian feel to those white men whose hands turned into dead fish when they had to shake a black person's hand. The men slithered about like lizards in polyester. They had forked tongues. They sat in their smug white churches, kept their tapless Sabbaths, sang their discordant songs, and took great comfort in the fact that they were better than anyone they knew and certainly superior to anyone they didn't know.

Although they were not allowed to dance, smoke, drink, go to movies, eat pork, fornicate, or let the mouth go below the navel, they did have racism, and it was their "truth." They drank their truth until it made them giddy. They drank to the dregs. They drank racism until it reeked from their pores. They drank it until they were rank, falling down, stinking drunk.

Racism was their drug of choice.

These strange and distant white men, who were genitally unkissed, intellectually sterile, and morally impoverished, told us that we, the colored people, were cursed by God. We were cursed by Noah. We were under the Curse of Ham. They told us that we, the colored, were to be hewers of wood and drawers of water. Servants. Forever. God Himself ordained it.

Much racial fear is predicated upon the fear of black bodies and black sexuality. Cornel West wrote in *Race Matters* that "Americans are obsessed with sex and fearful of black sexuality . . . fear is rooted in visceral feelings about black bodies and fueled by sexual

myths about black women and men." Sex and race were intertwined, twisted, and squeezed into our bone marrow, then dug up
and wrung out in movies, in the media, in myths, stereotypes, laws,
lies, and violence.

West goes on to state that "White fear of black sexuality is a
basic ingredient of white racism." And what better, more comfortable way to be genuinely racist and sexually insane than for it all
to be a part of God's Omniscient Plan.

A Fundamentalist Sex Education

At age seventeen I fled my hometown because people were beginning to notice and/or suspect that I was attracted to girls. In church
I flinched when the "sergeant" drilled me, as I sat bobbing and
weaving like a fighter trying to avoid the blows. I left to attend an
all-black theological Southern college built for the "colored" in the
1890s by church missionaries. There I was supposed to metamor-
phose into a heterosexual. There I was to meet and marry a ministerial student. (I couldn't be a minister, for only men were worthy.) I would write his sermons, though, and I would be straight,
and everything would be okay.

At the white theological colleges, the girls had to be in by 11:00
p.m. At the black college, the girls had to be in by 10:00 p.m. At
the white colleges, both male and female students could go downtown on the same day. At the black college, the girls could go
downtown only on girls' day, and the boys could go only on boys'
day. At the white colleges, males and females could sit together in
church, while that policy had just started at the black school. It was
obvious that the blacks were to be on a tighter rein. Nothing personal. Just obvious.

In my junior year the dorm mother announced that the following Wednesday's worship was going to be "special." She wanted

all of us to be there. She clued us in that the topic began with the letter *S*, and, most telling of all, no men would be allowed.

At last! Someone was going to talk about SEX! We were all excited. That Wednesday the dorm chapel was full of young women waiting to hear someone talk openly and unashamedly about sex.

There was a slight buzz and an audible titter in the room as Mrs. Fleming, our fearless leader, stepped up to the podium and said, "Ladies, please pay close attention. Tonight we are going to talk about something that affects all-l-l-l of us." She nodded with a knowing look. We nodded back. "It is something that we all-l-l-l need." I agreed. "And what is that?" She smiled conspiratorially. "That's right, it's SLEEP!" She went on to say how important it was to get eight hours of sleep, blah, blah, blah.

It was rather apparent that Mrs. Fleming and the administrators had chickened out, deciding that either they or we could not handle talking about sex. It was not mentioned or hinted at ever again.

At home, the church-led sex education consisted of a denomination-produced film of a young white couple readying for that first momentous kiss (after the obligatory six-month waiting period). At the end of the film, as the couple leaned in for the kiss, the minister's wife immediately slapped her hand over the camera lens, just in the nick of time to prevent us from seeing (potential) naughty parts meet. If we were actually to see two of the tiredest people on earth kiss . . . well, she wasn't going to be responsible for us going to hell in a handbasket! After all, sexual arousal could lead directly to atheism. Just like they told me that wearing a "natural" hairstyle would mean I didn't believe in God.

Back on campus, my attempt to lead a heterosexual lifestyle lasted for about five minutes. There were two major obstacles: (1) I met the ministerial students and was frightened by their obtuse stupidity, and (2) I met Michelle.

It was like a dream sequence. Michelle floated by me in a blue coat with a red collar, and said, "Hi baby." At that moment I kicked in the stained-glass window, decked the drill sergeant, and regained both my heart and soul.

I was in love.

With the campus sweetheart.

At a Christian fundamentalist theological college.

In the South.

In 1966.

To be gay on a Christian campus is to be in exquisite pain. One becomes a thief—eager to steal a glance, a furtive look, a lingering thought, anything to be with, near, breathe the same air as your beloved. It is to hide the fluttering heart, slow the loud pounding, stifle the sunlight of the smile, capture the kisses that never fly to cheek and put them in a jar, along with your aching, dying heart, on a shelf, behind a book, in a corner, in the dark.

One becomes a sexual charlatan, a sexual chameleon, a sexual comedian.

It is to become a danseur, tiptoeing on a high-wire, holding a tiny umbrella, high above earth, balancing precariously between heaven and hell. The safety net is called heterosexuality, but the hole in the net would hold the galaxy Andromeda, and if you fall . . .

It was Michelle who broke the news to me that Martin Luther King Jr. had been killed. I had known him personally. I was part of his "welcoming committee" to Los Angeles and had raised money for the cause. I loved him.

We were just a few hours from Atlanta, but they wouldn't let us leave the campus to go to the funeral. Too dangerous. Too much happening. The whole world had changed, turned upside down and inside out with no air to breathe. Two days after the funeral, I went to the grave site and took some still soft putty from the crypt and cradled it. I left part of my goodness, my innocence, my hope, right there at the grave.

Two days after Martin Luther King Jr. was buried, the church had its first integrated conference in Atlanta. Paul Harvey spoke. Two days after Martin Luther King Jr. was buried, the alien, reptilian, fish-handed, strange white men walked like ghosts past us, through us, as if we weren't there. As if we didn't exist. As if Martin Luther King Jr. had been a ghost who haunted their dreams and was gone forever so they could live in peace with their precious, sacred evil.

Two days after the end of the world, Paul Harvey, the radio commentator, spoke at our first integrated conference. His topic was, "The Mop, the Broom, and the Hoe." It was we colored folk who were destined to be tied forever to the mop, the broom, and the hoe.

Real Life Catches Up with Real Lies

My college years provided a rich background for my work as a therapist, but it had nothing to do with the academic training I received. Instead, classes were punctuated with such useful homilies as "Take the DE-Devil of Depression and Press On!" The full sweep of human passion, pain, promise, and paradox evident to me on a daily basis was denied, hidden by the sexual hypocrisy and the sexual fascism that permeated the culture of the church.

On graduation day as I walked back to the dorm in cap and gown, my teacher/professor/mentor, Dr. F., asked me to stop by his office. He congratulated me, complimented me on my achievements, and acted nervous. Before I knew what was happening, he grabbed me and kissed me, saying I wasn't his student any longer. I left hurriedly, confused and shocked. I went back home, wonder-

ing what that was all about. Within a few months of my graduation, the very married Dr. F. flew to Los Angeles to get on his hands
and knees, begging me to have sex with him.

Then there was a respected minister who taught Bible courses
at my college. He once said to me, "Uhmm, you have beautiful
limbs my dear." I got an A when I sat in the front row. The next
semester I purposely sat in the back to avoid his eyes. I got a C for
that term.

The president of the school was having sex with a seventeen-
year-old student. Everyone knew about it, even the president's wife.
The president went so far as to move the young woman into his
home to live with his wife and family. The dean of students was a
major closet case who went across town to pump and squirt with
the boys from the "worldly" college. Girls at the school who got
pregnant were humiliated, disgraced, and kicked out, sent home
in great shame and profuse tears. The boys who got them pregnant
merely went back to class the next day. No problem.

Billy, the son of my church's minister, had formed a Lay Activities Club at the school. Traditionally, a lay activities group would
offer Bible studies and engage in Christian endeavors in the community. But Billy's lay activities consisted of him and his group
"laying" every girl they could find.

And what happened to Michelle, my true love? She married a
ministerial student and became a minister's wife. We kept in touch
for years, until one day on the phone she launched into a rabid,
homophobic snit. She lambasted homosexuality, threatened me
with the fires of hell, and said, "I want the Lord to prick your conscience." I yelled into the phone, "I don't want a prick in my conscience or anywhere else!" Then I hung up in her face.

I left the church at age twenty-five because I could no longer
function as a healthy, spiritual being in an organization that was
racist, sexist, and homophobic. Right before I left, the minister

whom I had admired the most told me that homosexuality was related to "mice eating" in the Bible. The preachers were getting more homophobic, the sexism was rife, and the racism was no better than that day in 1957 when a visiting white minister assured us that "when I get to heaven, I'm going to find out where you people are and sit down and listen to you sing." Yet the weekly ritual of being with women dressed so beautifully for church, trying to be good, trying to be perfect, left me with an unending attraction to what I call "BBBs"—Boinkable Bible Babes. I just can't help it.

Forms of Fundamentalism

I have been out of the church and openly gay for twenty-three years, and over the years I have run into many fundamentalists. Many of them were old friends. What I found is that most of them are stuck in rigid belief systems that have made them virtually immune to logic.

I quizzed my old boyfriend from church when I saw him the other day. I asked, "If the world is only six thousand years old (which is a fundamental fundamentalist belief based on the Genesis creation story), then how do you explain dinosaurs?"

He replied, "Adam and Eve were seventeen feet tall!"

I asked, "What has that got to do with anything, especially dinosaurs?"

"Well, I'm just talking off the surface of my brain," he said.

Even my childhood friend, whose minister husband twice approached me for sex, told me recently that "homosexuality is a habit." I couldn't talk to her about her husband's "habit," which included beating her to a pulp when he felt like it. Being in denial, she wouldn't discuss it. She was also still in denial about her own father: a big-time, small-town closet queen.

What can you say to people who don't read nonchurch materials, don't know how to think critically, and lead virtually unexamined lives? Even my new hairdresser, an "ex-gay" Christian fundamentalist, feels that "homosexuals are led by an evil spirit and are recruited into the homosexual lifestyle."

Although there are countless ways to be a "fundamentalist," I have observed three distinct groupings or personality types:

1. The Great Controllers. Usually male, these fundamentalists operate on a public, often national level. They stoke the fears of their congregations and/or television audiences in order to obtain enormous personal wealth, power, and political clout. With fire-and-brimstone sermons they rail against women, militant homosexuals, liberals, abortion, feminism, and anything that might go against male dominance and authority. Some of them are apparently working out private demons in a public arena. Many of them have severe character and personality disorders. They seem to be driven by an overwhelming need to control people on a large scale. That which they cannot control, they wish to destroy. They are male supremacists, whose eternal enemies are women, gays, and independent thinking.

   The best way to deal with them is to monitor their attack plans, expose their real agendas, and, most important, meet them head-on with spiritual power and moral force.

2. The True Believers. These fundamentalists are the ground troops who follow the Great Controllers. They send in their money faithfully. They get on school boards and wreak havoc. They fight against sex education that tells the truth. They are offended by the theory of evolution. They want to ban any and all discussion of homosexuality in the classroom. They ban and censor books. Not all True Believers get as involved in reworking the world to their image, but most believe that American

culture is drowning in a moral sinkhole and can only be sal-
vaged by the absolutes of the Old Testament.

In terms of sexuality, one of the problems that the Great
Controllers and the True Believers have is that "the enemy" is
internal. By projecting their sexual fears and anxieties onto
others, they demonize homosexuals, homosexuality, and female sexuality. But it is these fundamentalists' own sexuality,
desires, and fantasies that frighten them. The enemy is within.

3. The Reluctant Allies. These fundamentalists are also true believers, but they realize that there is more than one way to exist as a fully functioning, loving human being. They are part
of the "movable middle" who may not agree with or understand homosexuality, but they wouldn't consciously hurt or
harm a gay person. However grudgingly, they can discern the
communality and basic dignity of others who are different
from themselves.

Sometimes there is a sea change in their attitude when their
son, daughter, best friend, or relative comes out of the closet.
Some of them get angry when they realize that they have been
lied to by the church about homosexuality. Some of them become our greatest allies.

Conclusion

It is important for us not to demonize fundamentalists in reaction
to their campaigns against gay rights. The struggles are fierce in
the African American communities in which I have lived, including my twenty-five years as a fundamentalist. For many, if not
most, religion is the anchor, the solid ground, and often the only
certainty. Church is the place for connection, both spiritual and
communal. It is up to us to remind people that religion should be
for healing, not harming.

Becoming a Cantor

JESSICA ROSKIN

I'm not sure when I decided to become a cantor. Perhaps I always knew I desired it, although I grew up believing girls couldn't become Jewish clergy, rabbi or cantor. Also, I was adopted at birth and grew up smashing all of the stereotypes of the Jewish "look" with my light blond hair, blue eyes, and little nose—becoming a cantor would be a way to prove to the world that I was, indeed, Jewish. All I knew for sure was that I loved music and I loved Judaism.

I was told that when my parents brought me home from the hospital in Miami on my third day of life, it was my father who carried me over the threshold of my new home. He walked straight across the house to the stereo, placed a set of huge earphones on me, turned up the sound, and declared, "*This* kid is going to grow up loving music!" Some of my earliest memories are of my father jamming on his tenor saxophone to a John Coltrane recording and of my being amazed that I could stick my entire arm into the instrument and still have sound come out. My father was a frustrated musician who played in a jazz band to help finance his way through law school, which his parents had expected of him. My existence gave my father the perfect opportunity to live vicariously through me. And it turned out I took quite well to it.

I was singing the moment I could talk and began taking piano lessons at the age of six. Teachers began to notice that I was a talented musician with an excellent ear. At the age of eight I joined our synagogue's youth choir, and my cantor, Irving Shulkes, recognized my abilities and took me under his wing. I loved listening to him, and as a regular temple-goer I memorized every nuance of the prayers he chanted. And when I finally became a bat mitzvah three days before my thirteenth birthday in May, Cantor Shulkes asked me if I would substitute for him during the summer months while he was away. The answer was simple. I sang in his stead for three years until I chose to spend my summers at Interlochen National Music Camp in Michigan. There I received my first real voice training. I had always wanted to take voice lessons, but area teachers turned me down, and professional vocalists strongly discouraged the idea. Apparently every teacher we came across said it was actually unhealthy to force growing vocal chords to sing "properly." It was best to just sing naturally until my body and therefore my vocal chords stopped growing. Yet Interlochen helped prepare me for the auditions I'd need to enter a music school for college. There was no question I would major in music.

That music school became Indiana University. Bloomington, Indiana, was such a culture shock in comparison to North Miami Beach, Florida. Everything was different. I had grown up in a neighborhood surrounded by Jews; now I was very much in the minority. I met people who had never met a Jew before, but according to them, I didn't look like one. It was a difficult adjustment.

I had grown up in the synagogue, but in college I felt the need to branch out socially and for the first few years felt that I didn't fit in at the Hillel, the Jewish presence on campus, so I stopped going. Hillel seemed like a group that wouldn't let you "belong" unless you spent all your time there. I wasn't ready to do that, and being a shy person, I was not outgoing enough to make friends. I would still celebrate all the holidays, but my friends and classmates weren't Jewish.

While I majored in piano, attending a university (as opposed to a conservatory) meant that I had to take courses to fulfill the necessary requirements to complete a well-rounded education. I used a roundabout method for taking the courses I wanted while still fulfilling my requirements to graduate. I took Hebrew and Jewish studies courses, part of Near-Eastern Languages and Cultures, which took care of my humanities credits. Over time I began to feel more comfortable at Hillel. Judaism remained an important part of my life. I think I needed to move away from Judaism for a time in order to realize how important it really was to me. I also finally took up voice lessons.

And then I saw the article. Many different people sent me this article during my sophomore year in college in 1987: "First Female Cantor Comes to South Florida." What's this? A cantor who's a *woman*? Is this possible? Suddenly, there was no question in my mind. There was nothing else for me to do. I knew the cantorate was for me. I learned afterward that there had been women in the cantorate since 1975, and I had never known! I don't believe I realized the importance of my decision at the time. I didn't yet understand it to be a "calling," although I also didn't believe it to be "a steady gig with a decent income." I just knew I could enjoy my chosen profession because it contained my two passions. I picked up Jewish studies as a minor, as I had already taken many of those classes, and began concentrating on my voice. At that time the Hillel rabbi asked if I would lead the entire Jewish population of Indiana University in worship as "cantor" for the High Holy Days, Rosh Hashanah and Yom Kippur. It was a great honor, and I took it on with gusto. I studied with Marco Rothmuller and learned how to chant a traditional High Holy Day service. I felt at home. It was a comfortable place.

It took five years and two summers, but I finally graduated with all the tools necessary to be a good candidate for becoming a cantor.

Even before I received my bachelor's degree, I flew to New York City to interview and audition for admission to the Hebrew Union College-Jewish Institute of Religion. It was an involved process. There were exams to check the level of my Hebrew language ability, an audition where I sang prepared music and sight-read in front of the School of Sacred Music faculty, and a psychological exam. I feared I wasn't good enough. But the acceptance letter finally came! I was moving to Jerusalem, Israel, to begin the first of my four years of study at seminary.

I had only been out of the country once, to Toronto, Canada. And now I was to move and live truly alone for the first time in my life in another country across the world from my parents and friends. It was a scary thought. The college's reason for having the first year in Israel is simply so students can learn the language. This meant that there were no dorms. We were expected to find an apartment and set up our utilities, shop for our food, and bank on our own. It gave us the opportunity to experience Israeli culture and to connect with the people. The school itself provided intensive Hebrew study beginning in the summer and continuing throughout the year. We also had a full course load. Jerusalem helped me to recognize all at once how truly insignificant I was and yet how important each human being is. I had grown up in a city where the oldest building was no older than Ronald Reagan. In Jerusalem I was walking on ancient and holy ground. You could live the history of the Hebrew Bible—it was all in Israel. A hotel was being built next to our school, and construction had to stop because the workers had unearthed a *city* and anthropologists had to be brought in to determine if it was a former civilization they needed to study further. Living in such an extraordinary place felt so spiritual. It helped me to realize that I was doing the right thing with my life.

Otherwise, Israel was not a wonderful place for me. The culture was so different than in the States. This might have been a time for me to finally feel like I "belonged." I was among my own people, and yet, once again, I looked like no one else. And this caused problems. I felt claustrophobic going outside. It seemed that Israeli men were always looking for blond-haired, blue-eyed women, and according to them, both American and Swedish women were looking for their dark, Semitic look. Their attention was unwelcome. One particular incident truly tested me. I had moved in with a fellow cantorial student about a week after she'd moved into her apartment. It seemed at first to be a great arrangement. Many of us, having arrived in the country and met our classmates, were doing some investigating. Who was married, who was single, who was attracted to whom, and so on. Well, my roommate was doing a lot of "exploring," and she was getting quite a reputation. Then came the day our landlord wanted to come by to pick up our rent check. When I told my roommate, she exclaimed she wouldn't dare be around, so I should be there when he came by. And when he did, I tried to hand him the check at the door, but he came in. And when I tried to lead him back to the door, he sat down and offered to write out a receipt for me. And then he tried to make a move, and when I resisted, he got angry and began to force himself on me. To this day, I don't know how I wasn't raped. When he finally left, I was a mess.

I ran to the school looking for my roommate but only found her when I returned. She was with a girlfriend. I told them both tearfully what had happened, and suddenly my world changed. She claimed that two days after moving into the apartment she had indeed been raped by the same man. My immediate reaction was to focus all my concern on her and feel lucky that I had not met the same fate. Our friend made us go to the school to speak with the dean, who called the rape crisis center. They arrived and said that although they understood I had been through a traumatic time, they really needed to concentrate on my roommate. I was beginning to feel like I wasn't receiving the attention I needed. And then I began to wonder. Why hadn't she told me? Why had she knowingly left me alone in the apartment to confront him? If she had in fact been raped, how is it she could so easily sleep with so many other men? I hated myself for thinking these things. I couldn't begin to imagine what she'd been through, so I did my very best to be supportive and not to think of my own problems.

The dean felt it was best to keep the story from the rest of the students and faculty. With the help of the rape crisis center, we made our way to the police department directly inside the gates of the Old City, where a female police detective took our statements. She took mine first, and it took a long time. It was then that my roommate began acting strangely, becoming intolerant of how long she had to wait and threatening not to give her statement. I couldn't understand her behavior. Once I had given the detective my story, she basically told me that in America we cried "rape" too easily and that my landlord probably just wanted to have sex with me and got angry when I resisted. It was the first time I recognized how different our culture was from Israeli culture. My roommate then gave her statement, and the police found our landlord and arrested him. He, too, gave a statement. He said he had thought I would be willing to have sex with him because the sex he had had with my roommate was consensual. When confronted, my roommate finally admitted that in fact their tryst had been consensual, and she'd lied about the rape. It was devastating news. So many things happened after that. I moved out of the apartment we shared, both to get away from the landlord and to get away from my roommate. She was asked to leave the school and therefore the country for the year, and she was told she could only return if she got psychological help. The only people who knew why she was leaving were the dean, the girlfriend who had helped us out, and myself. No one could understand why she would leave for no apparent reason.

I had never felt truly taken care of during my ordeal, and once my roommate's real story came out, the dean admitted to me that he didn't believe my story, either. I convinced him otherwise, but it was such a harrowing time, I wondered how I would get through it. I believe in the end it somehow strengthened me. I also considered myself lucky that I ended up having the opportunity to move back to the States earlier than expected. I was no longer happy in Israel.

A little more than halfway through the year the strife in Israel worsened, and suddenly we students found ourselves deciding whether or not to leave the country. There was a threat of war and attacks with missiles containing nerve agents like mustard gas. Israeli army soldiers came to our school to teach us how to seal a room in our homes in case of a gas attack, how to wear gas masks, and what to do if we were exposed to a nerve agent. We were each given a gas mask, a powder to put on an area of skin affected by mustard gas, and an EpiPen auto-injector in case we had been exposed to gas. It was a scary time. The school had a bomb shelter that was considered so good (our teachers called it a "five-star bomb shelter") that we didn't need to wear our masks while in it. Little of this mattered. There was much fear. And then war was declared; the Gulf War had begun. I flew home, with only one piece of luggage, on the last airline seat that existed. I realized we couldn't study or take our usual classes. Life had stopped for us in Israel. The potential for dying was too scary to contemplate.

Back in the States, the school didn't know what to do with the few students who had left Israel. They had never experienced this before. There was no existing program for first-year students in the United States. A decision had to be made, and soon.

The New York branch of the school quickly began to put together a curriculum. They didn't know how long it would take, so all students were expected to remain in or near New York City. I couldn't go home. I had no place to live and for a while no classes to attend. I felt displaced. My life and my belongings were in Israel in my apartment, my home and my parents were in Florida, and I was in limbo in New York City. My boyfriend's parents were kind enough to take me into their home in New Jersey, just over the George Washington Bridge. And I waited until Hebrew Union College developed the coursework necessary for me to receive a proper education. It was a difficult time of waiting and wondering.

Once classes resumed, I began looking for a place to live. I found a one-bedroom apartment with a roommate in Greenwich Village. She had cordoned off half the living room and made it her bedroom. But it was walking distance from the school, and so I moved in. I made new friends and got to know the faculty of the New York campus. Things calmed down. I applied for a student cantor position and got one at a synagogue in Connecticut.

I flew back to Israel in April, after the Gulf War ended, picked up my belongings, took care of the business of breaking the lease on my apartment, and said good-bye to my teachers and friends. I felt a myriad of emotions. I was excited to see my classmates again and to see the beautiful country Israel is. But I was nervous about cutting my lease short. By the time I returned, I did not feel that Israel was my home. I knew I belonged in the United States. I finished out the year in New York.

The next three years followed suit. I moved to a one-bedroom single in Park Slope, Brooklyn, attended classes, and on weekends traveled to my respective student congregations, my second and third years in Waterford, Connecticut, and my final year juggling two congregations, one in New York City and one in Manchester, New Hampshire. Each one provided me with a wonderful opportunity to learn, through experience, what it was like to be a cantor. It was the first time I felt really accepted as a woman, a Jew, and a cantor. It felt great! There were no questions asked, and I felt well prepared for any future position I would take.

As my graduation and investiture neared, I interviewed and auditioned with numerous congregations who were looking for a cantor. I took my first position with a congregation in New Brunswick, New Jersey. I had married a man I'd met on a blind date, and he and I found a place to live near my new congregation. Suddenly I came to realize that no matter how many student pulpits I'd had, they were nothing like working full-time: visiting hospitals, teaching adult education courses, directing several choirs, officiating at funerals and weddings, and tutoring kids. It was such fulfilling work, yet it was so constant. I felt less prepared than I had before I graduated, but I was excited at the opportunity to learn. I remained at that congregation for five years and felt I'd done all the growing I was able to do there.

In the interim, I had divorced and remarried, and my husband and I moved to Birmingham, Alabama, so I could take my new position at Temple Emanu-El. This place remains my home.

I have been a cantor for ten years now. I've learned so many things. I've learned that being clergy in the South is mostly a good thing. Southerners love their clergy. Religion is important in the South. We are seen as leaders in our communities. I was nominated for and am a member of Leadership Birmingham and spent a year learning about all the positive and negative that Birmingham has to offer. I have come to recognize that each person can make a difference in the lives of others.

As clergy we have the opportunity to do great things and make a big difference for good. And because of Birmingham's history of civil rights, clergy regularly meet with one another to continue dialogue and to work together to pass on the message of tolerance and compassion to our congregations. I am the current president of the Southside Faith Communities, a group of clergy and religious leaders in a specific area of downtown Birmingham. We meet regularly to learn about each other, and we are working to form a committed group for making positive change in our area and in our greater community. I am also a member of the Interfaith Leadership Institute of the National Conference for Community and Justice, a program that allows me to work with other clergy in the faith community to make changes in our own religious communities as well as our greater Birmingham community.

I can look back now and know that there was so much to learn and that I'll spend a lifetime continuing to learn more about my cantorate and myself. I still have a long way to go. I hope to continue to grow and mature personally and professionally, to learn more about myself so that I can feel like a whole person, and then carry that on in my work to my congregation. It will be a lifelong process, and I look forward to that process. I'll have setbacks along the way. I have come to recognize that as a spiritual leader, my responsibilities to my congregation never cease. The friends I make in the congregation are still my congregants. I can never fully separate my personal life and my professional life. These lessons can be difficult and sometimes painful. When I was that thirteen-year-old girl on that pulpit in South Florida, I never could have imagined what this profession meant in terms of touching people's lives and being involved in "community." In college, when singing at High Holy Day services, I realized I could touch people with my voice, but I couldn't imagine what it meant to take the prayers of my congregation and sing them to God on their behalf. It's a daunting responsibility, and I take it seriously. I am proud of what I have accomplished and strive to do much more in the years to come for my community, my congregation, and myself.

I Lead Two Lives

Confessions of a Closet Baptist

MAB SEGREST

I wrote this essay almost twenty-five years ago, at thirty, to describe the contradictions in my life over working in a profession that I loved and living freely accepting my lesbian sexuality—a negotiation that required huge trade-offs that I articulated as being "terrorized into staying in line" for fear of losing both a job and a vocation. Three years after it was published, I left the ultraconservative Baptist institution and teaching itself, unable to sustain such profound compromises to my personal and intellectual integrity that academics in the early 1980s for many lesbians seemed to require. Leaving teaching broke my heart, and (as broken hearts often do) opened me up to other possibilities. I made a "career shift" and became an antifascist activist and community organizer. I helped to form a statewide network to oppose Klan and neo-Nazi activity and hate violence. Memoir of a Race Traitor, *published in 1994, narrated the lessons of those years. Then I worked through the 1990s with the World Council of Churches.*

Three years ago, I returned to college teaching full-time. Changing careers again—in my early fifties—felt perilous, and I was not

*sure the academy would let me back in, given the density of femi-
nist academic work over the previous decades and the barriers that
some kinds of feminist theory raised between "community" and
"academy." I took a one-year position as acting chair of gender
and women's studies at Connecticut College in New London, Connecticut, in 2003. The next year I applied for and was offered a
permanent position, then I was promoted to full professor and
given tenure. Connecticut College has domestic partner benefits,
which means among other things that my partner, Barb, and our
daughter, Annie, are on my health insurance policy. Last year the
Connecticut legislature passed a bill establishing civil unions. For
three years now, I have traveled back and forth from New London
to Durham, where Annie and Barb maintained our permanent residence and Annie finished up high school this year. I've been surprised how much I have appreciated being outside the South—a
sentiment underlined by the "blue" that marked Connecticut and
other New England states in last fall's presidential elections.*

*I am back now to doing the "work that I love best." I get to look
out each week on a sea of young faces, "watching eyes focus and
unfocus as words register or float out the back window—every period the necessity to generate interest, every hour a hundred tiny
failures and successes." I am moved by this generation—which is
the generation of my daughter Annie, young people coming to maturity during the "war on terror"—by their strengths, their vul-
nerabilities, and their beauty. I am happy to be teaching them even
as I continue to learn with them how to give my life each day to
what I love, not to what I fear.*

I lead a double life. By day I'm a relatively mild-mannered English
teacher at a Southern Baptist college. By night—and on Tuesdays

Footnote: The student whom I call "Fred" in this essay died of AIDS within the
decade.

and Thursdays and weekends—I am a lesbian writer and editor, a collective member of *Feminary*, a lesbian-feminist journal for the South. My employers do not know about my other life. When they find out I assume I will be fired, maybe prayed to death. For the past four years my life has moved rapidly in opposite directions.

When I started teaching English at my present school, five years ago, I knew I was a lesbian. I was living with Sue, my first woman lover. But I wasn't "out" politically. I had not yet discovered the lesbian culture and lesbian community that is now such an important part of my life. The first time I had let myself realize that I was in love with Sue I sat under a willow tree by the lake at the Girl Scout camp where we both worked and said aloud to myself in the New York darkness: "I am a lesbian." I had to see how it sounded, and after I'd said that, gradually, I felt I could say anything. When, three years ago, Sue left to live with a man, I knew my life had changed. I read lesbian books and journals with great excitement. I joined the collective of *Feminary*, then a local feminist journal, and helped turn it into a journal for Southern lesbians. I started writing. I did all this while working for the Baptists, feeling myself making decisions that were somehow as frightening as they were inevitable. Early issues of *Feminary* record the process. First there is a poem by "Mabel." Then an article by "Mab." Then the whole leap: "Mab Segrest." I knew if I could not write my name, I couldn't write anything. I also knew: if I can't be myself and teach, I won't teach.

It is fall as I write this, and September brings back memories of new plaid cotton dresses, clean notebooks, pencils sharpened to fine points, and especially a stack of new books full of things I didn't know yet. Since my junior year in college, over a decade ago, I have wanted to be a teacher. For a long time—before Sue and I both made the brave, reckless leap that a woman makes when she loves another woman for the first time—teaching was the most important thing in my life. I have always liked school. And I always—

always!—loved to read. During my childhood—which if it was full of small-town life and summers with my brother in the woods near the lake was also full of the deep loneliness of being queer—I spent many hours with books on the front porch swing or in my father's chair by the gas heater. I have always pondered things in long conversations with myself walking home from school, my hands slightly waving as I held forth to some invisible audience. Now in my classes I love the challenge of looking out over a sea of consciousness, watching eyes focus and unfocus, as words register or float out the back window, every period the necessity to generate interest, every hour a hundred tiny failures and successes. Teaching is the work I love best. I can bring much of myself to it, and much of it into myself. But as a lesbian teacher in a society that hates homosexuals—especially homosexual teachers—I have learned a caution toward my students and my school that saddens me. The things my life has taught me best I cannot teach directly. I do not believe that I am the only one who suffers.

The first time homosexuality came up in my classroom it was a shock to my system. It was in freshman composition, and I was letting a class choose debate topics. They picked gay rights, but nobody wanted to argue the gay side. Finally three of my more vociferous students volunteered. I went home that day shaken. I dreamed that night I was in class, my back to my students, writing on the board (I always feel most vulnerable then), and students were taunting me from the desks—"lesbian! queer!" The day of the debate I took a seat in the back row, afraid that if I stood up front *IT* would show, I would give myself away: develop a tic, tremble, stutter, throw up, then faint dead away. I kept quiet as my three progay students held off the Bible with the Bill of Rights, to everyone's amazement, including my own. (I certainly knew it could be done; I just hadn't expected them to do it. No one else in the class had figured any legitimate arguments were possible.)

Then the antigay side rallied and hit on a winning tactic. They implied that if the opponents *really* believed their own arguments, they were pretty "funny." I called an end to the debate, and the progay side quickly explained how they didn't mean anything they had said. Then one of my female students wanted to discuss how Christians should love people even when they were sick and sinful. I said the discussion was *over* and dismissed the class. The only time I had spoken during the entire debate was in response to a male student behind me who had reacted defensively to a mention of homosexuality in the army with, "Yes, and where *my father* works, they castrate people like that." I turned with quiet fury— "Are you advocating it?" All in all I survived the day, but without much self-respect.

The next year, on a theme, a freshwoman explained to me how you could tell gay people "by the bandannas they wear in their pockets and around their necks." She concluded, "I think homosexuals are a menace to society. *What do you think?*" A pregnant question, indeed. I pondered for a while, then wrote back in the margin, "I think society is a menace to homosexuals." I resisted wearing a red bandanna the day I handed back the papers.

Sometimes friends ask me why I stay. I often ask myself. I'm still not sure. A Southern Baptist school is not the most comfortable place for a gay teacher to be—sitting on the buckle of the Bible Belt. A few years ago Anita Bryant was appointed a vice president of the Southern Baptist Convention. I stay partly because teaching jobs are hard to come by, especially in this vicinity where I'm working on *Feminary.* I have begun to apply for other jobs, but so far without success. I wonder how different it would be in other places, where bigotry might be more subtle, dangers more carefully concealed. Mostly I stay because I like my students. They remind me, many of them, of myself at their age: making new and scary breaks from home and its values, at first not straying very far and needing to be told, "There's a bigger world. Go for it." Teaching them is like being a missionary, an analogy many of them would understand.

Two years ago I came out for the first time to a student. I had resolved that if any gay student ever asked me to identify myself, I would. So when Fred came up to my desk before Christmas vacation, sporting one new earring and wanting to talk about bars in Washington, I knew it was coming.

"Where do you go to dance?" he asked. (At the time, there was one gay disco in the vicinity.)

"Oh," I evaded, "you probably wouldn't know it. What about you?"

"Oh, you wouldn't know it either." Then, quickly, "It's between Chapel Hill and Durham."

Me: "I think I do. It starts with a C?"

Him: "Yes. You go there?" His eyes lit up.

Me: "Yep."

Him, politely, giving me an out: "You probably just went one time and got disgusted?"

Me: "Nope."

By this time the class was filling with students, milling around my desk and the blackboard behind us. I suggested to Fred that we finish the conversation after class. We did—in the middle of campus on a bench from which we could see anyone coming for at least half a mile. I felt a sudden sympathy for the CIA. He asked me if he could tell his friends. I took a deep breath and said yes. But they never came to see me. I still don't know how far word had spread; every now and then I have the feeling I exchange meaningful glances with certain students. I would like for gay students to know I am there if they need me—or maybe just to know I am there—but I do not take the initiative to spread the word around. I have made the decision to be "out" in what I write and "in" where I teach, not wanting to risk a job I enjoy or financial security; but it is not a decision I always feel good about. I see the unease of most college students over sexuality—whether they express it in swaggering and hollow laughter over "queer" jokes or in timidity or in the worried looks of married students from back rows—and know that it is part of a larger dis-ease with sexuality and the definitions of "men" and "women" in this society. I see how they, and most of us, have been taught to fear all of our feelings. And I understand all too well, when I realize I am afraid to write—to even know—what I think and feel for fear of losing my job, how money buys conformity, how subtly we are terrorized into staying in line.

The closest I ever came to saying what I wanted to was in an American literature class last year. Gay rights came up again—I think I may have even steered the discussion in that direction. And a student finally said it to me, "But what about teachers? We can't have homosexuals teaching students!" I resisted leaping up on the podium and flashing the big *L* emblazoned on a leotard beneath my blouse. Instead, I took a deep breath and began slowly. "Well, in my opinion, you don't learn sexual preference in the classroom. I mean, that's not what we are doing here. *If* you had a gay or lesbian teacher, he or she would not teach you about sexual preference." I paused to catch my breath. They were all listening. "What he or she would say, *if you had* a gay teacher, is this . . . " (by now I was lightly beating on the podium) " . . . don't let them make you afraid to be who you are. To know who you are. She would tell you, don't let them get you. Don't let them make you afraid." I stopped abruptly, and in the silence turned to think of something to write on the board.

And if they ever *do* have a lesbian teacher, that is exactly what she will say.

Interview with Lee Smith

SUSAN KETCHIN

When Lee Smith was a little girl, she gave God a tea party. Perhaps remembering that, she told me she was relieved when she learned that I would be interviewing Harry Crews; until then, she said, she'd been concerned that her interview would be the most "heathen" one in the book. Such good-humored worry about piety and heathenism is emblematic of Lee Smith's utterly engaging personality, how she greets and is greeted by the world. Of medium height and build, with blond hair and light blue eyes, a radiant smile, and Scots-Irish fair skin, Smith is noted for her generosity of spirit, quick wit, and completely unaffected, easy manner. A native of the small mining town of Grundy, Virginia, she speaks in a clear, mountain accent, telling stories with an ironic twist, a self-deprecating joke, or a pinprick at pretentiousness. In describing her genuine struggles with religious belief and morality, she says, "I'm so much *not* New Age."

An extraordinary number of friends from every part of the country and from all periods of her life still come to see her. On vacation at a friend's summer house in Maine, she sits at the kitchen table, looking out over the lake and mountains beyond, and writes funny postcards (one card that pictures a moose grazing in the foreground, a little apart from the herd, gets the caption: "Married moose dreaming of the single life").

Recently, Lee Smith teamed up with the Tarwater Band (a folk trio who named themselves after the backwoods prophet in Flannery O'Connor's *The Violent Bear It Away*) for a combined reading/ concert in which she read from her latest novel, *The Devil's Dream*, and the band sang original and traditional mountain tunes from the book, such as "The Riddle Song" and "Shady Grove." Introducing a passage, she confessed, "I always wanted to write a story in which God speaks; in this one, He not only speaks, but sings."

Lee Smith claims that she cannot sing (or even keep rhythm), but all who know her know that she sings beautifully through her work and her life, with a feeling, a clarity—and a wallop—that is as extraordinary and as comforting as corn whiskey and wild honey. Throughout my interview with her, she talked with a lively sense of humor about her life and work. A keen listener, observer, and storyteller, Smith spoke openly and poignantly about her impassioned religious sensibility as a child, how in her beloved mountains God and nature were one, so that her "whole childhood was really full of God and wonders."

On a warm June day we sat drinking coffee on a chintz sofa in Lee's downstairs den. Bookshelves lined the entirety of one long wall; her writing desk sat in a corner between the bookshelves and the gray brick fireplace on the wall opposite us. Sliding glass doors provided a pleasant view out over thickly wooded land. The day was balmy, clear, and breezy, like many June days in these parts; the tulip poplars and oak trees were budding with new green leaves, providing rest for our eyes as we talked.

Let me begin by asking you about your religious sensibility and its origins. Flannery O'Connor once wrote that she always admired believers who came to the faith as adults because she would find it difficult to believe in some of the more mystical tenets of her faith without having been "brung up to it." How were you "brung up" to your religion as a child in Grundy? Do these experiences show up in any of your fiction? One way to approach this might be to talk about Karen, in "Tongues of Fire."

"Tongues of Fire" in a way is truly one of the most autobiographical stories I have ever written. The family is all made up, but the character of Karen is absolutely the way I was as a child, including the obsessive reading, and the obsessive religion. I was raised in a little church, the Grundy Methodist Church, that was very straight-laced, but I had a friend whose mother spoke in tongues. I was just wild for this family. I would have gone to live with them if they'd let me. My parents were older, and they were so overprotective. I just loved the "letting go" that happened when I would go to church with my friend.

And then later, I got a boyfriend who was a member of another church. This was a *wild* church. And I would go to the revival with him and be saved—constantly. So religion and sex—you know, excitement, passion—were all together. I couldn't differentiate between sexual passion and religious passion. This was what we all did on dates, was go to the revival. It was a turn-on.

Things were done very literally. One thing they did at that church that I'll never forget, was that they had a big ply-board thing, in the front of the church, full of lightbulbs. This was at regular church. If you were present, you and your family, you'd go up and screw in your lightbulb. And it would turn on. And over the top of the whole thing, it said, "Let Your Little Light Shine." And if you weren't there, it would be so obvious to everyone else in the congregation because your little light would not be shining. Something about that, I don't know—it was the only thing that was happening for me in terms of excitement.

You were saved several times?

Yes, I was just given to rededicating my life and being saved. All this was an embarrassment to my mother. I was a Methodist, and I had been sprinkled as a baby. I was perfectly saved as far as she was concerned, and she wished I would quit going to these other churches and "acting up." You know, it was a "low-class" thing to do, in my mother's eyes. But even in the Methodist Church, which I went to, and MYF, and church camp every summer, and retreats, I was—more so even than Karen in the story—a very religious child. A *very* religious child. I was such a religious child that I used to think that I heard God speaking to me. In fact, I still think I may have. I mean I'm not putting that down. Because I was an only child, and I was by myself a lot of the time, and I did a whole lot of nonstop praying, reading the Bible, thinking, and so on. I loved Joan of Arc, and I loved these inspirational stories like Karen does.

Nature particularly inspired me. For instance when I was at camp, several times I was absolutely sure that I heard God, or saw a vision, or whatever. I'm sure there could be a psychiatric word for the kind of little child I was.

I was also given to rituals. Like before I went to bed at night, I had about twelve things I had to do. The door had to be cracked a certain way because there was a witch in the closet. The light had to be a certain way, this and that. I was always prone to imaginings.

Did this passion last throughout your girlhood?

Yes, up through high school—all the time I lived in Grundy. I would go to youth revivals. I would speak at youth revivals—up until the time I went away to school to St. Catherine's [a preparatory school for girls in Richmond]. St. Catherine's was Episcopal. I'm telling you, all that stuff, that institutionalized ritual, just knocked it out of me. It deadened all the passion. Somehow, in the town I grew up in, I associated religion with a kind of a life force. Then all of a sudden at St. Catherine's, since it was an Episcopal school and it had all these rules, I began to associate religion with a death force. I guess it's fair to say I outgrew it; I got interested in other things. It was one of those things of childhood.

Do you feel sometimes that you miss it? Or was it somehow a relief to go beyond it?

I was sort of glad to outgrow it because it was wearing me out. It was becoming clear to me that I was getting to be at an age that I would have to do a lot more with it, or just give it up. Because with me, I've always been, unfortunately, an all-or-nothing kind of person. I still feel that way now. I feel like, okay, if I want to start really going to church again, I'm going to have to really go.

I've heard you mention that before—that you'd have to be involved completely if you should ever think about becoming involved again. It is as if there aren't any restraining forces, that you must go whole hog.

Yes, anything I'm in, I get completely into, and for that reason, I think I have held back. I think it is because I was that kind of a child. I was so completely wrapped up in it. You know, I associated it with nature, and I was a real tomboy. We played in the mountains, all the time. And it was like the whole world of my childhood was really full of God and wonders. But as you get older that sort of thing scares you because there are not any boundaries. It was terrifying. So I think in a funny way, I was glad to hit St. Catherine's, and all those rules, and all that mumbo jumbo.

The ritual did seem to kill any joy; it's a "kill-joy." Though you felt that need for ritual in your daily emotional life as a child, the institution managed to overdo it. Was it a matter of overkill?

It was for me in terms of religion. After that I pulled back. I still have the sense of it, and probably someday I will have to find that again. I have a feeling that it's out there. I associate it with the mountains. At some point I'll have to move back to the mountains, I think. At some point I'll have to throw myself into it all again.

Have you ever been to any black church services? The times I've been able to throw myself into things and even be transported have been at black revivals.

Yes, as a matter of fact I just heard Jesse Jackson in Atlanta, last Saturday. Just the way the crowd is! Yes, being transported is something that I have always both desired and feared. More than anything else. It's what used to happen to me as a child, but it's what's scariest to happen as an adult, because as an adult, you have to be responsible. You know, I can't be transported. I have to go to the grocery store.

Yes, and I have to be back by three to pick up the kids.

I can't have a religious experience; I have to be back by three. All these people are depending on me. I did feel a sense of being lifted up at Jesse Jackson's sermon; everybody was holding hands, swaying. That was a wonderful time.

You know, I think it's significant that your sense of being carried away as a child was so sensuous, so concrete. You felt closest to the spiritual in the mountains, in nature. Everything was all of one piece rather than the spiritual being divorced from the physical and confined to an institution, a church, a separate place. In the usual idea of what it means to be religious, church is where you go and are asked to renounce the physical world as being the source of temptation and sin. You're asked to separate the physical from the spiritual, at least the sensual from the spiritual.

I surely did have that sense at the Episcopal Church. I did associate that renunciation with all the rules at St. Catherine's. When I went there, we had so many, many social rules.

It's as if some churches fear the physical so much that they feel they have to build a containment vessel for it, like they do for a nuclear reactor.

And strangely enough, I married somebody who had a similar experience. Jim Seay had been the most religious boy in the world, in Mississippi. In fact, he had gone to a Bible college, Mercer College, and even when he was as old as twenty-one, he was going to be a youth minister, and he went to Ridgecrest every summer. But he had stopped all that by the time he got to Ole Miss, fairly late, in his twenties. When I married him, he, too, was threatened by the consuming power of his religion, didn't want to fall back into it. He did not go to church, did not want to go to church, did not want anybody else to go to church. Maybe if I'd married somebody who was a churchgoer, I would have learned how to maintain a balance. Or seen how I could be religious and not have it take over my life. But as it was, for a long time, I didn't have anything to do with the church.

Yet, oddly enough, I was writing about it all the time. Except in my work, I didn't want anything to do with it. [Laughter] But I was always thinking about it.

Except in one of the most important areas in your life, your creative work.

Right, exactly. But I mean in my daily life, I just shied away from it.

I understand that so well. I had a similar experience growing up. And here I thought I was the only one. Have you ever read The Spiritual Life of Children *by Robert Coles?*

No, I have not. But I want to.

It presents with such respect accounts of the spiritual lives of these youngsters who talk quite openly and lucidly about their own spiritual lives and what we've been talking about. It's very moving to read.

And it's all real.

I think one reason it's so real is because for these children, religion involves their whole body, along with the whole mind and spirit. They do not have the capacity or the desire to compartmentalize the experience. And, as you said, you still feel a mixture of desire and fear, you still feel you have to "contain" yourself. Ironically, this only demonstrates that you are an intensely spiritual person.

Well, I have never gotten away from this ideal, this notion—I take it seriously. I'm always worried about what's the right thing to do. It's so hard to figure out in the real world what is the right thing to do. What is good? I struggle with it all the time. I spend a lot of time thinking about it. It's just old-fashioned morality, I guess.

It's making a genuine effort to know, to understand, to do what's right.

Yeah, I think we all have to make the effort.

There are some people who don't do that.

Yes, they just don't think it's anything to worry about. And you know, my whole notion of morality runs counter to the "Do your own thing, follow your bliss" idea. I'm so much *not* New Age.

What do you think of Joseph Campbell?

I love Joseph Campbell's ideas on religion and culture. I love to think in terms of comparative religions. I think Joseph Campbell is very much a moralist. But a casual reading or a casual interpretation of his theories does lead to a very hedonistic, New Age kind of thinking that a lot of people are following that I don't think he ever intended.

Some people might find a way to make any statement self-serving and hedonistic, in any case.

What they're looking for is more of a justification of what they're going to do anyway.

This intensity, and passion, and your need to achieve a balance—

Yes! I'm still working on it. I believe in God, I've just never been able to find a way to act on that without having it take me over.

I'm scared I'll be taken over. I need to find a church somewhere, some way to be able to act on it more without feeling I'll be engulfed.

Caught up in the whirlwind.

Yes, I see it as a whirlwind, I really do. Also, as I get older, more and more, I see the importance of the church in the community. I was against the institution of the church for two reasons for a while—the Episcopal Church was so deadening with its rituals, and the primitive church that had turned me on so much as a girl, well, they put down women. Therefore, as an adult, I still need to find a church that doesn't put down or stamp out things that I believe are basically good. It's something I struggle with all the time. Maybe I'll just die struggling with it and never get it reconciled. But it's real important to me.

It's a very painful thing, isn't it?

It's very real.

You mentioned something about it being something you've needed to pull away from, except in your writing. How do you think this struggle is played out in your writing?

I don't know. I'm not very articulate in talking about my writing. I'll say one thing, I'm one of those kinds of writers who writes a lot. I have written a lot ever since I was a girl. I write fiction the way a lot of people write in their journals. It's only several years later that you go back, read through your journal, and see what's going on. I go back and read my fiction, and see what's going on. *Fair and Tender Ladies* is so much about the struggle we've been talking about. And Ivy is like me; she is unable to find a religion that suits her—an organized religion. She makes up her own. Writing for her is sort of like it has been for me—a sort of a saving thing. Almost a religion of its own.

Writing is a kind of salvation?

Yes, as a way to get in touch with that intensity, a way of getting in touch with and staying true to me. I do feel, when I'm writing at a fever pitch, that intensity that you feel when you get saved. There's nothing else that makes you feel like that. There's getting saved, sex, and writing. Those are the only things I know of. [Laughter]

That pretty much says it all. Except, of course, chocolate pecan pie, which some people say is better than sex.

It might be! But anyway, Ivy struggles with those things, with the only religion she is exposed to, her mountain church, in the same way that I struggle. And she dies without finding God in the traditional sense. And I might too.

For Ivy's people, her community, religion is a serious matter. It evokes extreme behaviors. From early childhood, it was a norm for you to think about good and evil, and when you'll be saved, will you go to heaven or hell. That is one reason I loved Karen, and Tammy's mother in "Tongues of Fire." The book I'm doing is a book about Southern religion as it's treated in Southern fiction. There may be some fascinating connection between being Southern and being compelled to come to terms with religion.

You do have to, if you grew up in a Southern community. You can't evade it. Now you can grow up in some place like Chapel Hill, as my own children have, unfortunately, and not really be exposed to religion and not be called into account for not knowing anything. There are plenty of children who are not regular churchgoers, these days, whose families are not, and it's no social stigma, or anything. But in Grundy where I grew up, when some family was mentioned, somebody'd say, well, they're Methodist, or they're Presbyterian, or they go to So-and-So's church, or whatever. In the South, if you grew up at the time when we did in a small community, you were exposed to it intensely as a part of daily life. It is still true in small towns; it's only not true in university towns, and in towns as big as Atlanta and Charlotte.

You know, when Karen got saved, over at Tammy's church, as she was standing there dripping wet, Tammy suddenly looked at her differently, as if a wall had gone up between them. What was that all about?

I think that Tammy herself didn't take all that "religion stuff" as seriously as Karen. It was just a part of the way her mother was to Tammy. Tammy could take it or leave it; but for Karen, it was a big deal. Karen was on a spiritual quest. Tammy wasn't. To Tammy, it was just something that embarrassed her.

When Karen was spending the night with Tammy, she saw Tammy's mother reading her Bible at five o'clock in the afternoon, during "gin-and-tonic time," as Karen says. This was a striking difference between the two families and cultures that she had never thought about before. That contrast in turn came to be a wall between the two girls. When I read the story, it struck me how very sad this story is. It is a story about loneliness and difference, the alienation, of many of the characters. It's one of the saddest stories I've ever read.

It's a real sad story. It's really sad what's happening to the father there. It's dealt with in a sort of ironic tone, but it's just terribly sad, what's happening.

Here we've got a brother well on his way to alcoholism, in a coma, almost dead, a mother who has no earthly notion of how to handle anything, yet she's "got her hands full," a father who is slowly having a nervous breakdown, a sister who is promiscuous, and thirteen-year-old Karen whose wonderful gifts and seriousness about life are going by unseen.

She's invisible, as she says.

Like the "Camp Spirit." Did you become invisible in your family?

I didn't because I was an only child and I couldn't. I think I wanted to. I was entirely too visible. Which was why I was glad to leave home. So the story wasn't autobiographical in that sense. Everything I did when I was growing up was remarked upon.

Every breath you drew. Especially in a small town, I bet.
Oh yes.

Who are some other characters in your fiction who are trying to work out their religious ambivalences?

I think Crystal in *Black Mountain Breakdown* is. And in *Oral History,* what Richard Burlage goes to the mountains for is to become less "Episcopalian," to loosen up. To listen. In a way he's sort of an autobiographical character. It's the notion that if you loosen up too much, if you become too spiritual, you go nuts.

You said that writing has enabled you to make some kind of resolution of your own ambivalences?

I continue to feel deep conflicts. But the link for me between my own religious feelings and creativity is that with writing, you go out of yourself—but you know you can come back. You won't stay stuck in the craziness.

Several writers I've interviewed have talked about a deep conflict between their own creativity and the church, both its norms and teachings.

Yes, for me there is a great conflict between the church and my own creativity, all the time. I knew from the beginning I couldn't write about sex or violence, not and expect to go back home. For instance, when the play *Fair and Tender Ladies* was performed in my hometown at the high school auditorium, people came up to Barbara Smith [the actress playing Ivy Rowe] afterwards and talked to her as if there were no difference between the character she played and herself, the real person. And for them, there isn't. There is no difference between the characters and the writer who created them, either. Some churchgoing people were upset with the sex in the play. You shouldn't write about it, you shouldn't act it out.

But I must be honest when I write, or else why write? So, I've got to write about *some* sex, *some* violence. And about religion. I mean, Jesus has actually spoken to me. It happened to me. When

I was young, about thirteen. I heard a voice and it said, "Lee." I think that's why I must write about it, we all must write about it.

Do you think that will remain true for writers and artists here in the South as it becomes, in Walker Percy's phrase, more "Los Angeles-ized"?

Oh yes, more so. I think religion is not dying out, but becoming more influential. You see more and more churches, more little churches everywhere. As a teacher, I see it more in my students.

Doris Betts describes herself as someone who consciously deals with Christian themes and images in her fiction. She says she tries not to hit you over the head with her beliefs, but instead to speak in a whisper, as one does in trying to get the attention of small children. Reynolds Price, too, has spoken openly about this dimension of his life and his writing.

Yes, and Doris and Reynolds Price are both great writers that way. I don't consciously think about those things. I do consciously go through rituals when I'm getting ready to write my novels. I read the Bible all the way through when I was writing *Fair and Tender Ladies*. Ivy did that, too. She hates a good part of the Bible. But she loves Ecclesiastes, where there is the passage about a time for everything. And, in fact, Ecclesiastes became the structure of the last chapter of that novel, and of the whole thing. I mean Ivy thinks the Bible has some "pretty good stories." But Ivy can't accept religion as being available to her—religion as it was taught to her in her mountain church was so antiwomen. Also, those early primitive churches in the mountains taught salvation by grace alone— and that's a problem for me. It just seems like another way of justifying frontier hedonism—for men only, that is, not for women. It seems like much of that kind of religion was instituted by men and conspired to hamper women.

You deal with some of that in The Devil's Dream, *don't you?*

Yes, very much so. There was always this split in the mentality of the culture, in its members. In the early days, some bands I write about even had two names, the gospel name for Sunday mornings and the honky-tonk name for Saturday nights. There was always a pull between the honky-tonk life and the church and home life. There were these huge polarities. One big conflict was how to be a star and keep Jesus. Often in these early days, when you got saved, you were given your "gift song," the song you sang when you accepted Jesus as your saviour and renounced your old life. All your music had to then be sacred music, dedicated to God from then on.

There is an old story I read about in the Southern Historical Collection [at the University of North Carolina], and I wrote about it in the new book. It's about a mountain girl who sang and played a fiddle. One day her father forbade her to sing any longer, saying it was "of the Devil." Grief-stricken, she goes mad and plays the fiddle on her front porch until she dies. It's a true story.

Where the Spirit Moved Me

JEANIE THOMPSON

Poems are rough notations for the music we are.
—Rumi, as translated and spoken by Coleman Barks on
The Rose (Maypop Press)

Stopped at the edge of the page. This is where I find myself. How to enter that territory? Who am I? Where am I? This is a place that I must enter through poetry, if I enter at all. Like Rumi's half-dazed sayer of poems, I know the light I am seeing is where I come from, but I stumble toward it, if I make my way in that direction at all.

In a poem from twenty years ago, I said it like this:

At the center there must be
something, I write. I cross out
"something" and write "nothing."
At the center there must be nothing.
At the center there is a particle
of light around which I focus

everything I've known or felt
and from this center move outward
into words.

I would like to touch you,
whoever you might be.

63–73, "Autumn Journal," *Witness*

Same voice, same attempt to find something but now there's structure—line, pacing, and that final statement, "I would like to touch you, / whoever you might be." You, the reader, are the person I am addressing. I, the writer, am the person I address.

Speaking of the spiritual in relation to poetry makes a kind of Möbius strip, for poetry is fundamentally a transcendent act. Poets are naturally spiritual practitioners. A poem locates the poet, as I try to say in "Autumn Journal," and simultaneously connects with the reader, creating a bond. Although this may not always feel spiritual, the method or mode of communication is to *connect*, to *touch*. This is the essence of spirit: to tell us that we are in touch with something outside of ourselves. And as Rumi says, poems are "rough notations for the *music* we are" (my italics); in other words, as humans and spiritual beings we are somehow *less rough* than poems, and in our best selves perhaps we *are* songs, music. This is a reversal of the usual notion of art transcending life. But if poems take us to the world of the spiritual and the divine, then we must abide in that realm some of the time to be able to recognize it.

Society usually relegates poets to the "odd" zone of folks, calling us out for special occasions like presidential inaugurations or to comment when things go really bad and three minutes of poetry on National Public Radio will help shape our chaotic thoughts. Most of the time poets practice what they do alone, in the quiet of their homes, cells, or pickup trucks. After the practice and the writing, the poems go forth into the world, for better or worse.

From what I know of the poetry writing experience after more than thirty years, poets try to understand the world around them and to *say that world* back to themselves in lines. In "448" Emily Dickinson says, "This was a Poet—It is That / Distills amazing sense / From ordinary Meanings—". I always return to that definition because I can see what she means—I mean literally see it: the poet, in the laboratory of language, creates a physical essence the way a perfume-maker takes the essence of the flower from the rose's petals and renders it ("amazing sense") to something so pure ("Attar so immense") that it can be mixed with a medium and later dispersed as fragrance so that we can experience the rose for ourselves.

Somehow, I've never felt there was a difference between my poetic utterances and my awareness of God. I reread that statement and think, "Where did that come from?" Yet I know it's true. God. Spirit. Self. Knowledge. This is the amniotic fluid a poet swims in, takes nourishment from, reenters to touch the divine. For every poet, the inspiration is unique. For me, it is often *place,* a physical space and time, with sensory details, that leads me to poetic utterance. It is a physical place, and yet poetry takes me there through *placement* in language. As a Southerner, I inherently trust place, I recognize it and return to it.

I was born in Anniston, Alabama, and raised in Decatur—a town in north central Alabama recognizable (outside the state) by its proximity to Huntsville—home of NASA before Houston and of Werner Von Braun. Rockets, high intelligence, and well-educated scientists. Snugged up to the foothills of the Appalachians, Huntsville is home to Monte Santo State Park, where my family picnicked in summers and we kids sailed in swings that seemed taller than any in flat Decatur—heard cicadas ringing in our ears louder than loud as dusk fell over the mountain and somehow felt a little closer to something better, more exotic, than where we lived.

I was at once close to the mountain cradle of my birth and among families who had migrated to this area to be a part of the 1950-60s brain trust that the industries and armed forces attracted to north Alabama. Science was in the air like a benevolent virus. But what did I feel drawn to? Language, words, saying things that made sense to me. At age fifty-two, the rhythms of Southern speech are still in my syntax, my word choice and inflection. These will never leave me. They tell me who I am by reminding me where I come from. Southerners carry a heavy blessing and curse—I call it "the duality of place." We love our homes but grieve the sins that stain us—racism, poverty, illiteracy, the slow acceptance of reform. Yet we always return to claim our birthright.

Mapping the Spirit

In what ways am I, a Southern woman poet, also writing of spiritual matters? It seems that is my *only* subject—what moves me, moves my heart, impels me toward some knowledge outside of myself, and pushes me toward acquisition of the transcendent. If I had to say the subject matter that I return to over and over, it would be *the workings of the human heart*. What else is there for a poet to consider? Spirit, the heart's workings, interlaces everything I do as a poet. I write of those I love, those I grieve for, those who've caused me pain, those I've hurt.

As the lover's touch foretells the journey into pleasure, that whiff of promised understanding through crafted language draws me in again and again. I choose to call this *spiritual experience*. And though I struggle with the fact that I may be supremely arrogant to think I can make a spiritual journey alone—and immediately turn to my bookshelves crammed with poetry, theology, nonfiction, drama, and philosophy as proof (these are my teachers and guides)—I believe that finally I must be willing to lead myself. And so I return to poems to tell me what I know.

When I consider the idea of writing *out of* place, being *placed in* language, it seems useful to look back at what I've written and see where it came from. In my head I make a mental map of Alabama and place on it the poems that occurred in a particular place—that emerged as a result of locale. It is a simple thing to do; it feels utterly familiar. I create my own literary map and through cartography, that favorite metaphor of poets, I can approach this assignment with some honesty.

I unroll the map and place large stones from Alabama's creeks on the four corners. Drop down and touch Decatur, Highway 67, on the backwater of the Tennessee River. "At the Wheeler Wildlife Refuge," a poem that led me to say, "What tells me I'm alive / is impossible, useless to carry away." This poem chronicles a visit to my youthful stomping grounds through the artificial construct of an observation building and walking trails created as part of a visitors' center at the refuge. I had returned to Decatur to spend a few days teaching creative writing to middle schools students, and this work had me in an image-making frame of mind. So here I was, tramping around the place I had known all my life and thinking about its components, listening to what people said, seeing birds that looked like black pepper according to a little girl who was waiting in line to use the observation telescope, hearing the rattle of sorghum plant stalks in the fall breeze, noticing how vines with-

out their leaves make a "ghost network" over everything. All sorts
of random fodder rattled around like imagistic BBs in my head.
Then suddenly I was struck with how this place told me who I was,
but I couldn't carry anything of it away as a token of identity, that
it was useless to try. And there was the poem. Shaping the physical
details, blending them with the revelation, working the nuances of
line in open form. This is my ritual of knowing. This keeps me in
touch with something outside of myself.

What moved me in the first place? Certainly it was the spirit of
home, the awareness of a visceral landscape that has importance
because it is the one I know. *Knowing* is what drives us. To know
ourselves, the world, the other, the divine.

Move forward in time and touch another spot on the map. The
strip of Highway 82 between Tuscaloosa in west Alabama and
Montgomery, the state capital. It was along Highway 82 that
"Litany for a Vanishing Landscape," a ten-poem sequence, came
to life around a series of questions that occurred to me while driving. I got them down as fast as I could, steering with one hand,
writing with the other. Later I asked photographer Wayne Sides if
he could photograph off of these images shaped as questions, and
he said, "Yes, but I don't want to just work from those lines, I want
to photograph in tandem with what you are doing." From this
grew the "Litany" project, a collaboration of poems and photographs and later other incorporated objects that told a story of the
disappearing Alabama landscape and the lingering spirit of place.

One very cold November day, riding out in Tuscaloosa County
with Wayne and listening to an Alabama football game on the car
radio, I found the poem "Lyrical Trees" emerging in response to
the landscape. Trees became dancers who "dream to imitate" and
the poem's final line breaks the image—and the poem itself—open
into the "shattering air." Here I was practicing the transcendent
again—word-painting the landscape but pushing the image to-

ward self-escape—the trees will rise out of themselves, as dancers dream about, and the air will take them—even as they are shattered out of themselves—and they will be transformed.

This is the essence of the lyric impulse. *The urge to move toward transcendence through image and metaphor.* The process where one comparison leads to another and another, and then the metaphor takes us beyond the equation of "this equals that" to a third thing—a synthesis of understanding that cannot be paraphrased but must be rendered in the medium of language.

Move ahead in time again to 1998 and locate east Alabama and the small community of Cusseta in Chambers County. During a political race we make a Sunday visit to a black church where the candidate for his fifth term in the Alabama House of Representatives, a man well known and admired, will make a brief appearance during the service. Taken by surprise at the authenticity of their worship, their a cappella opening music, I am swept away from the exigencies of politics into something that feels achingly universal—the sounds of slave songs rising about our heads in 1998—out of the mouths of church elders. "At Mt. Nebo Baptist Church" is the result, a poem that uses run-on, unpunctuated sentences in an attempt to capture this moment. I had to begin the poem in the rural landscape, with a box turtle, joe-pye weed, a hawk, before I could move inside the church. The poem ends with transcendent forgiveness—again, I was impelled by the place toward a point of understanding. Too soon that day I was wrenched awake from the awareness and thrown back into the corporeal grind of seeking votes. But the poem remains as a token that something real happened to me in that place. If no one had ever read that poem, if it had never seen the light of print, it would remain a private relic that I had experienced a spiritual renewal in that moment in time.

A wise poet once suggested to me that *the poem is the interface between the inner world of memory, spirit, and emotion and the outer, sensual world.* I know I feel most alive when I touch that moment of illumination that foretells understanding and I apprehend the interface. It seems this is the mystic's way, and as a poet I accept my tiny role in spiritual practice that may serve as a step on the path toward understanding for a reader. But I should be clear that I write to get these moments *right* even as they are the closest thing to an experience of God's presence. Poems give me a window into the divine—whether they are my own or someone else's. All the great teachers, and certainly Jesus Christ, the one with whom I am most familiar because of my Western upbringing, speak in metaphors to teach people truths. Read the New Testament and you hear the voice of a passionate poet, driven to get it across to his followers through language—parable after parable. Perhaps those Bible lessons I received regularly as a young child were the most formative in my poetic development. Some long forgotten Sunday school teacher painted a vivid picture for me that it *is* possible to make metaphors that will lead us out of our dark misunderstanding and into a bright, sensually populated realm of truth.

Touching the Spirit in a New Place

For a number of years I have made a study of place in Southern literature. I've listened to writers discourse on it, I've written a bit about it, and I've been deeply aware of it in my own poems. When asked to talk about myself as a spiritual writer who is also a Southern woman, I turned immediately to place. So, what happens when I go to a completely new place, halfway around the world?

In the summer of 2004 I spent two weeks based in Vence, France, working with the Alabama artist Nall on a book about his work and, among other things, the influence of his Alabama upbringing on his art. Set in the region known as Provence-Alpes-Cote d'Azur, Vence is an ancient, walled city dating back to before the first century and was considered an important Roman town. From its central, historic core a modern town has grown through the centuries. It is situated close to several of the perched villages, including the fortified city of St. Paul de Vence. Walking in Vence with my hosts the first evening of my arrival, I was giddy with recognition—I felt beyond any doubt that I was walking in a familiar landscape, the same streets, shops, sounds, and smells. I had met this landscape before in dream.

The dream I call the "dream of the creative" has recurred for about ten years, though I am sad to say I have dreamed it less as I have tried to analyze it. Generally it occurs during a time of creative stimulation—not necessarily when I am writing, but when I am in contact with other artists or particularly inspired by a place or a richness of things. The motif is always that I am moving toward the interior of a city, that I cross a clear demarcation line—it can be stepping over a curb, jumping down from a wall, or entering a street. I am aware that the place I've entered is the center, is a place I've longed for. Sometimes the dream presents narrow streets with shop after shop of things to eat, see, or touch. Often there are restaurants, places where I know I can enter and eat fascinating things and see interesting people. For a while I thought that the seven years I spent in the New Orleans French Quarter provided the imagery for this dream, but then I walked in Vence and realized it was ancient France that I must have been dreaming about.

It was deeply calming to assimilate this recognition. I wanted to blurt it out right away, but something told me to hold on to my revelation—not to cheapen it by jabbering about it in my jet-lagged state. As Nall and Tusica and I walked to the café for dinner, we went along narrow streets, made unexpected turns, passed small shops, and finally came to Le Clemenceau, their favorite café for pizza, located in the dead center of town. Here I was, in a restaurant where the food was known to be good and the proprietor a genuine friend. I quietly pondered this in my heart as we ate.

About a week later I told Tusica, and she said, "Well, I know where we must go today. Then you will truly be in your dream!" So we made the short drive due west along a two-lane mountain road to the little town of Tourrettes Sur Loup—we walked the quiet, cobbled narrow streets, peered into a few shops, bought some stone jewelry, and lunched at a small café. I photographed one street, and as I look at that photo now, I am looking straight into the entryway of the dream of the creative. If this was not a spiritual experience, I don't know what that means. I was touching a place that I knew was part of my history, perhaps all human history. Whether I had lived another life there, whether I simply felt communion with souls who had, it was bigger than my one life, and it included me with love and grace.

My job, as a writer, is to help you, the reader, see this place, experiencing it as fully as I did—perhaps more so. That is the challenge I accept when I write. I haven't written poems about this experience—perhaps taking the information in is all I can do for now. I know the poem is there, waiting, though perhaps reluctant to emerge until I can give it what it needs.

Where the spirit moved me is impossible to chart—no map can really contain it, of course. Even pointing to locations and saying, "A poem happened here on such and such a day because . . . " doesn't begin to explain what gives the poem a spiritual quality. Looking at the poems of place, of illumination and understanding that I return to, I would have to say that I find a significant grounding, a rootedness in place that is close to spirituality. Like Dylan

Thomas's famous opening line "The force that through the green fuse drives the flower" that sets up a series of comparisons between energies in man and the forces in nature, I feel a force, kin to spirit, that drives the poem to a kind of flowering. If the poem is any good at all, the reader gets to experience that revelation.

A favorite poem of my own is called "Snapshot in the Red Fields," written as a prose paragraph presented in alternatingly indented lines, with run-on, unpunctuated sentences. The third person "speaker" is a cotton farmer, passionately alive in his red fields. In fact, the act of plowing overwhelms him so that he thinks it is something no one, not even his wife, could understand:

> [it is] impossible to explain to her,
> to anyone, how the fields keep him alive, and at these moments, when
> the plow has turned the rows and the earth is open before him
> in its deep
> moist iron-rich splendor, he would just as soon dive into it and forget
> himself, down, down into its depth, rather than ever lose it or
> know
> that the season would not come again

8–13, "Snapshot in the Red Fields," *White for Harvest: New and Selected Poems*

I conjured this farmer after riding through plowed cotton fields that opened out on either side of Highway 20 running east and west in north Alabama. Overwhelmed by their beauty, I had to find a way to give human emotional value to them. My character wants to return to them, as if returning to a lover. Beyond the hardscrabble of eking out a living as a cotton farmer, a miserable existence in many ways, there is a spirit in the land that transmits to him. I wanted to feel that too—and to render it for you, the reader. My reward was in the writing, pure and simple, but there is reciprocity—writer to poem / poem to reader.

As with most writers, the spirit moves me to write when I am open to it. Like love that finds us when we least expect to be found, spirit of place lingers. As a poet, I know that seeking the spirit, telling of that quest in a story or metaphor that you, the reader, can share, is my continual joy and sweetest challenge. Signaling, "When to turn and feel that presence pass through us / [and] to know that we are changed—whether to blossom / or to flood—we are changed" remains my appointed task in the world's work.

A Baptist-Buddhist

JAN WILLIS

It was the kind of slow-motion thing that you see in movies. My car was skidding, swerving out of control on the slush and ice of a highway recently plowed—but not recently enough. I was returning from Boston, trying to get back home to Middletown before the big snow-and-ice storm forecasted for later that afternoon arrived. Now I knew that I should have taken my hosts' advice and stayed in Boston.

The storm had been the delight of weather forecasters for days, and I did not want to be caught in those treacherous driving conditions that had been their theme all week. Leaving Boston on the Mass Pike around 7:00 a.m., things had seemed all right. I put on some music and applauded myself for making the right decision. After driving for about an hour, the flurries began. It was a beautiful thing, snow; and I'd soon be home. By the time I turned off onto I-84, the roads were getting bad. Attempting to calm myself, I determined that if I slowed down, keeping ample space between my car and the ones in front of me, I'd still make it okay.

Just after passing Hartford, the snow got really heavy. I cut off the music and gripped the steering wheel a bit tighter. At least now there were only three lanes to worry about, not the five that had led into the Hartford area. Traffic slowed but was moving. I told myself, "Only twenty minutes. Then home." I tried to keep focused on the cars ahead and the tracks they were making. "Follow in the tracks," I told myself. "Keep inside the tracks. You'll make it." I was scared.

Then suddenly I saw things from the perspective of an observer. The car was spinning out. It turned almost sideways then, suddenly, righted itself. Then it began to slide toward the center guardrails. I silently mused, "So, this is how it is. Just like that, one's last moments." Images of my father and sister flashed by. No time to say anything to them. I saw the guardrails rushing toward me. The car would hit them in the next second and that would be it.

A booming *OM MANI PADME HUM!* woke me up. I was screaming the mantra at the top of my lungs. I saw myself leaning forward, clutching the steering wheel so tightly that my knuckles were white. My car had moved back into the tracks of the middle lane. I don't know how it got there. In less than a split second, it had simply jumped back into the tracks of the lane, as if some giant invisible hand had snapped it up and placed it down again.

I looked to my rearview mirror. Behind me, cars were braking and swerving. They had been attempting to stop as they saw me careening into the guardrail. I said another few *OM MANIs* for them while I held tightly to my steering wheel.

As I continued on, now moving very slowly, I thought more about that near brush with death—how quickly our treasured selves can be extinguished; how fragile life really is. And I thought about how surprisingly that booming *OM MANI* had come out of me, in what I thought was my last moment of this life. It is the mantra of Avalokitesvara, the Buddha of Compassion. I regularly intoned it whenever I passed a dead animal on the highway, to wish it peace and blessings. Perhaps in those compressed seconds I saw myself as a dead animal. The best I can figure, however, is that it was the shortest prayer I knew. What went along with it, I think, was the wish not to be separated from Lama Yeshe in whatever future rebirth. Perhaps I was a Buddhist after all.

Once, when I was teaching at UCSC, the car I was driving suddenly stalled less than a foot from a railroad crossing. The next second a speeding train roared by, its warning horns blaring, while my car trembled and shook as though it would fly away. Then, I had not called out the mantra. At least I didn't think I had.

And, returning one night to Hartford's Bradley Airport, after two lovely Christmas holiday weeks spent with my family in Alabama, another thoroughly frightening event took place. I was, as usual, flying on Delta Air Lines. The company's biggest hub is Atlanta; they fly hundreds of flights into Birmingham, and their pilots have a first-rate flying record. Hence, for most of the flight into Hartford, I was feeling pretty relaxed. However, temperatures all up and down the East Coast were pretty frigid, and this caused a good deal of turbulence. As we bumped along, dipping and rolling in the rough air, there were more than a few white knuckles in evidence. Buckled in at my window seat for most of the hour-and-fifty-minute trip, I tried to maintain a relaxed attitude, trusting in our pilots to steer us safely in. Still, as Bradley's airfield came into view, I found myself being more than a little relieved.

From the window, I could see the lights of the tarmac. Like most others on this particular flight, I let out a giant sigh of relief. Seated beside me were an older woman who had seemed frightened for most of the trip and a young girl who was, presumably, her grandchild. I smiled encouragingly before I spoke, "Okay! See, there's the runway! It won't be long now."

We were no more than a few feet above the tarmac. The plane's landing gear was down, its headlights illuminating the field. Then things abruptly changed. In an instant, the plane veered steeply upward. It went into a climb that was almost perpendicular. We were like astronauts, our heads pressed back against our seats, our bodies feeling the g-forces of liftoff. My own knuckles went white. Papers from somewhere started blowing through the compartment. Overhead doors snapped open. Oxygen masks dropped. Some people started to scream. I started to pray, at first aloud and then silently, but speeded up, with urgency. I called on both my guru, Lama Yeshe, and upon Jesus. "Lama Yeshe!" I screamed. "May I never be separated from you in this or future lives!" Gripping my armrests in silence, I continued, "May you and all the Buddhas help and bless us now!" Without pausing, I then fervently intoned, "Christ Jesus, please help us. Please, I pray, bless me and all these people!"

That plane climbed straight up for almost four minutes. My prayers became continuous mantras. Finally, the engines' roar lessened and the plane began to level off. The pilot's voice came over the speakers. He sounded nervous himself but tried to speak reassuringly, "Ah-h, ladies and gentlemen, I'm sorry it's taken so long to get back to you. It seems that just as we were landing we hit one of those stiff wind shears, and we had to get out of it. We're going to try this landing again, this time from the east." A collective sigh went up from all of us.

I call myself a "Baptist-Buddhist" not to be cute or witty. I call myself a "Baptist-Buddhist" because it is an honest description of who I feel I am. When I was on that plane, racing straight upward through the frigid night air, I did not feel as though I were simply hedging my bets. I felt sheer and utter terror, and I called on both traditions for help. Long ago, Kierkegaard had argued that one doesn't know what one really believes until one is forced to act. That climbing plane showed me what I believed.

Most times, actually, I think of myself as being more an African American Buddhist. When I seek to make sense of things or to analyze a particular situation, I am more likely to draw upon Buddhist principles than Baptist ones. But when it seems as though the plane I'm on might actually go down, I call on both traditions. It is a deep response.

About this dual description, my folks seem, generally, accepting. Though one day while telling me that she thought my years with Lama Yeshe hadn't caused me any harm, my mother did let me know, in subtle and not so subtle ways, that she worried for my soul and its salvation. Many others, who've had occasion—or taken the license—to comment on it, have stridently voiced disdain and disapproval: "Either you believe in Christ, our Lord, as your sole and only savior, or you're lost!" A young, well-educated, and articulate black man who was visiting Wesleyan once told me exactly this. To this vociferous attack by a newly reborn Christian, and to others like it, I can only say, "Well, I trust that Jesus Himself is more understanding and compassionate." The Jesus I knew from the Gospel stories was the Jesus who had ministered to women, to the poor and downtrodden; and He was the Jesus I knew personally, because He had ridden with me on that bus ride to Cornell [to attend college in 1965]. Moreover, it seems to me that those who see a disjuncture in my being a Baptist-Buddhist haven't spent any amount of time reflecting on what, or who, a Buddha really is—or a Christ, for that matter. As always, in matters of faith and of the heart, a little concrete experience and practice usually takes one higher, while at the same time sets one on firmer ground.

If I have learned anything about myself thus far it is that in my deepest core I am a human being, graced by the eternal truths espoused both by Baptists and by Buddhists. And more than that, I am aware that it is not any particular appellation that matters. For ultimately, what I have come to know is that life—precious life—is not a destination. Life is the journey.

Afterword

When I climbed into Sister Frances Mason's green Impala, no one knew where my mother was. She'd gone missing. But I wasn't worried. I'd gone with her when she left the time before, and we'd only walked a few blocks to the Birmingham Motel. Daddy came every day, and while I did cannonballs off the diving board into the bluest water I'd ever seen, they talked. Within a week, we went back home. I don't know what the problems were or what promises were made, but I knew Mother had been real sick. I assumed that's why she cried a lot. Sister Mason, the interim pastor for the Wesleyan Church at the top of Chestnut Street where I lived, must have been aware. She volunteered to pick me up so I wouldn't have to walk to church, something I'd gotten used to doing since VBS the summer before. Sister Mason's hair was silver; so were her bifocals. I figured the glasses were special; after all, she could see the Holy Spirit. Every Sunday, she covered her clothes with a shiny satin robe that had a long, dark collar and climbed into the pulpit to preach to the same twenty faces. Even though I couldn't see the Holy Spirit, I could see that the Holy Spirit did something to her. God's love, she cried, was undeserved, his grace a gift too overwhelming for words. So she wept them instead. Her arms seem to float upward as she called out in choked gratitude, then she challenged us to follow in Jesus' footsteps. Back then, I didn't know where the footsteps went. But I've always loved a challenge.

After the service, she drove me home. It was almost dark, and lightning bugs were everywhere. Instead of stopping in front of my house, she stopped next door at my grandparents'. She must've known Mother had been found and was now resting in their extra bedroom. Not only did she bless me as I climbed out of the Impala, but she gave me a novel to go with my New Testament—*Black Beauty.* Is it any wonder my understanding of spirit and story and suffering get all tangled up?

Mother lay beneath one of Bigmama's quilts, the green brocade bedspread folded at the foot. The curtains were pulled.

"Let's go home," I told Mother after showing her the book, but she told me she couldn't go yet, even though home was only two hundred feet away.

"She's hurt," Bigmama said, and pointed to Mother's ankle.

"What's the matter," I asked.

"You go on now. It's time for bed. Maybe start on that book. Your mama needs to rest some more."

I did as I was told. I clutched my New Testament in one hand and *Black Beauty* in the other—the good book and the new book—and went outside. Two steps up. Across the driveway. Down the sidewalk. Onto the front porch. I guessed someone would be there, maybe Daddy or my older sister. But I didn't go inside. Instead, I stacked the books and gripped them as tightly as I could, one hand on each side. Then I let them swing through the air, just beneath a lightning bug. The dim, yellowish light fell toward me for a moment, before it recovered and flew away. I stood beneath another light and swung the books again. Again the light fell, recovered, and flew away. I could make the little lights dance. And so I did this for a long time. I swung and swung and swung until my arms finally gave out.

When I got older, a boy showed me how the light could be torn off the bug's belly and worn on the finger like a ring. But that kills the bug, I protested. It's just a bug, he said. It was true: the light did make beautiful jewelry, and I had squashed my share of bugs. Yet I couldn't bring myself to rip out a single light. When he offered, however, I took his without hesitation. It didn't last long. The light faded before I got home.

I didn't know whether Mother's ankle was twisted or whether it was broken. But I couldn't help wondering. Would she wear a cast or an ACE bandage? I hoped a cast. I couldn't sign a bandage. But what would I write? And why didn't they tell me what was wrong? I wanted to know. I think that's why I spent so much of my life trying to figure out what was wrong with other people. And surprised that when I told them, they weren't grateful.

Then, I couldn't understand what a wounded spirit was. Now, I know that depression is a complex diagnosis, and it can take root and bloom wildly in certain gardens, especially Southern ones. My mother, grandmother, and I were told we should be Godly women, Southern ladies, selfless wives and mothers subjecting ourselves gleefully to the men around us. The mold was exact. And exacting. For a woman whose shape didn't fit, she was supposed to keep trying, to keep bending, even if it meant she would break.

I reached a similar point when I neared the age Mother had been back then. I, too, wanted to run away, wanted to rethink the place I'd come to consider home, though by now I knew the hurt wasn't confined to a single bone. I did wonder, though, if something inside me wasn't twisted or broken. I'd been in a women's Bible study at my next-door neighbor's house discussing a book, *Inside Out*. My mother-in-law, a Godly role model extraordinaire, asked us twentysomethings, Are you where God wants you to be? Apparently God had everyone but me right where He wanted them. I was the only one who said no.

And yet I was doing all the Godly woman things: I was a stay-at-home mom with two beautiful daughters, leading Vacation Bible School and attending church on Sunday mornings, Sunday nights, and Wednesday evenings. I even had a new ironing board. What could possibly be out of place? I got some strange looks from the group after my honesty and felt like I was a huge disappointment to my mother-in-law. The study continued, but I didn't hear anything else. A roar had started inside that felt maddening. I went home determined to fix better casseroles, maybe even cross-stitch. Surely if I did more domestic-y things, the noise would go away. But it didn't. And no other proper spiritual women seemed to hear it. Maybe I wasn't as proper as I thought. I changed churches hoping this would offer solace. The new church had a special room for mothers to breast-feed their babies, programs to help stay-at-home moms stay at home, and a social clique for homeschool mothers that made junior high cliques seem tame. Women there got celebrated mightily, as long as they didn't teach adult Sunday school, or try to be church leaders, or speak out at will. I twisted and twisted and bent and bent until I hardly recognized myself anymore. And the noise only grew louder.

I finally hit a point where I couldn't continue anymore. Was I breaking? I joined a creative writing class, where we didn't study Bible-based books, but we were all studying redemption in ways that felt truer than anything I'd felt since Sister Mason and her church on Chestnut Street. For me, salvation had been a certain belief formula that depended on getting outside myself, a sort of anti-self set of rules that might protect me from, or cleanse me of, myself and my sinful tendencies buried inside; but in this class, for the first time, I had to go inside myself, below the roles I'd taken on as layers, to the source of all that noise: my own voice.

I'm still the little girl challenged by Jesus' footsteps. And I still swing books with everything I've got because it makes light dance.

But when it comes to diagnosing the twisted or broken, I gave up. I believe what matters more is the healing, however it comes.
—WR

At St. Mark's Episcopal Church in Little Rock, Arkansas, in 1973, the male minister who taught our confirmation classes used the pronoun "She" to refer to God. This was shocking and exciting. I was a thirteen-year-old feminist in favor of the Equal Rights Amendment and wore a pro-ERA button when I served as a page in the Arkansas House of Representatives. A few years later, the Reverend Peggy Bosmyer became the first female Episcopal priest in the Diocese of Arkansas. "Reverend Peggy" was young, vibrant, energetic, and serious about her ministry. I got to know her in EYC activities and as a leader of the "Search for Christian Maturity" weekends. At the same time, I was attending a Catholic high school for girls run by the Sisters of Mercy, and there again it was clear to me that these women who had chosen a religious life were strong, powerful, in charge. One young African American nun we called Sister Freddie had obtained her law degree and had chosen to wear what the nuns called "street clothes," instead of the habit. So as a teenager I was surrounded by positive, and politically progressive, images of women in the church.

As I grew older, went to college, and entered my twenties, religion slipped away from me—or I from it. My church, which had once been a kind of comfortable second home, seemed irrelevant to the concerns of my young adult life, getting married and entering the work world and forging my own identity, an identity that aimed more for the bohemian intellectual than for what I then saw as the bourgeois complacent. Because I connected my spiritual life solely with church, I let that go, too, apart from a few iso-

lated incidents that didn't seem to fit together into anything co-
herent. It was only when I was in my mid-thirties and my mother
became seriously ill that the issue of spirituality came up again. It
was not just the big questions—why is this happening to her? can
prayer help her heal? what does faith mean when the cancer is
pronounced terminal?—but a growing awareness of the spiritual
realm that brought me back to thinking about my relationship to
the divine and to the world around me, about finding community
with others who seek to honor the spiritual aspects of our human
nature. I remember small moments of grace, as when my mother,
partially paralyzed by a stroke, unable to feed herself, and near the
end of her life, woke up one morning smiling and told my sister
and me, "I'm quiet in my spirit." Theodore Roethke writes that,
"In a dark time, the eye begins to see." That was my dark time.
An inner eye reopened.

I began to pay better attention. Mostly I read and wrote in my
journal. I started to wonder how the creative life and the spiritual
life connect, and I found sociologist Robert Wuthnow's *Creative
Spirituality: The Way of the Artist*. In this book, which has been a
wonderful source of understanding and reflection for me, he writes
of how a number of the artists he interviewed for his book see
themselves as being on a spiritual journey filled more with questions than with answers. "Different views notwithstanding, there
is often an emphasis in artists' remarks on questioning prevailing
assumptions. They want people to see that spirituality is not removed from ordinary life but infuses it, even to the point of being
part of the human body and the created order."

In the past ten years, I have, in various ways, including sporadic
church attendance, sought to find ways to nourish my spirit, and I
am now, and probably always will be, still seeking. When Wendy
asked me to collaborate with her on this collection, I jumped at

the chance to further explore how other Southern women, some of them artists, have found a spiritual path that works for them. What strikes me most is how diverse these paths are, how much room there can be, when we have the courage to claim it.

—JH

Contributors

SHIRLEY ABBOTT is the author of *Womenfolks: Growing Up Down South* and *The Bookmaker's Daughter: A Memory Unbound,* which was a *New York Times* Notable Book. Born and raised in Hot Springs, Arkansas, she now lives in New York and Massachusetts.

DOROTHY ALLISON was born in Greenville, South Carolina, and makes her home in northern California. *Bastard Out of Carolina,* her first novel, was one of five finalists for the 1992 National Book Award. It went on to win both the Ferro Grumley and Bay Area Book Reviewers awards for fiction. The novel has appeared in translation in French, German, Greek, Spanish, Norse, Chinese, and Italian. A movie version of *Bastard Out of Carolina,* directed by Angelica Huston, premiered on Showtime in 1996. Allison's second novel, the critically acclaimed *Cavedweller* (Dutton, 1998), was a *New York Times* best seller. *Cavedweller* won the 1998 Lambda Literary Award for fiction and was a finalist for the Lillian Smith Prize.

VICKI COVINGTON lives in Homewood and teaches creative writing at the University of Alabama at Birmingham. Her novel *The Last Hotel for Women* was converted for the stage by her brother, playwright Randy Marsh, and was performed before sell-out crowds. It was also selected by the University of Alabama Press for reprint in their Deep South series. Vicki's works include *Women in a Man's World, Crying; Cleaving; Last Hotel for Women; Night Ride Home; Bird of Paradise;* and *Gathering Home.*

Susan Ketchin (interviewer of Lee Smith) is a musician and university teacher who has been teaching Lee Smith's work for many years. She is author of *The Christ-Haunted Landscape: Faith and Doubt in Southern Fiction,* which includes interviews with Lee Smith and eleven other writers about the origins of their faith and their literary imagination.

Sue Monk Kidd is the author of two widely acclaimed nonfiction books, *The Dance of the Dissident Daughter* and *When the Heart Waits.* She has won a Poets and Writers Award as well as a Katherine Anne Porter Award. Two of her short stories, including an excerpt from *The Secret Life of Bees,* were selected as notable stories in *Best American Short Stories. The Secret Life of Bees,* her first novel, was nominated for the prestigious Orange Prize in England.

Cassandra King has published three novels, *Making Waves in Zion, The Sunday Wife,* and *The Same, Sweet Girls,* as well as stories and essays in various quarterlies and anthologies. She has taught college writing classes, conducted corporate writing seminars, worked as a human interest reporter, and published an article on her second favorite pastime, cooking, in *Cooking Light* magazine. A native of LA (lower Alabama) she now lives in the low country of South Carolina with her husband, Pat Conroy.

Barbara Kingsolver's ten published books include novels, collections of short stories, poetry, essays, and an oral history. Her work has been translated into more than a dozen languages and has earned literary awards and a devoted readership at home and abroad. In 2000 she was awarded the National Humanities Medal, our country's highest honor for serving through the arts.

FRANCES MAYES is the author of three best-selling books about Italy. The number one *New York Times* best seller, *Under the Tuscan Sun,* remained on that list for more than two years. It was followed by the memoir *Bella Tuscany,* also an international best seller. In 2000 she published *In Tuscany,* a collaborative photo-text with Bob Krist and her husband, the poet Edward Mayes. A widely published poet and essayist, Mayes has written five books of poetry, most recently *Ex Voto* from Lost Roads Publishers. Her previous books of poetry are *Sunday in Another Country, After Such Pleasures, The Arts of Fire,* and *Hours.* She is also the author of *The Discovery of Poetry,* published by Harcourt. Formerly professor of creative writing at San Francisco State University, where she directed The Poetry Center and chaired the Department of Creative Writing, Mayes now devotes herself full-time to writing. Her first novel, *Swan,* was published in October 2002, and she edited the *2002 Best American Travel Writing.* She and her husband continue to divide their year between San Francisco and Cortona, Italy. The film version of *Under the Tuscan Sun* (Disney/Touchstone, Fall 2003) features actress Diane Lane.

DIANE McWHORTER'S book about Birmingham, *Carry Me Home,* won the 2002 Pulitzer Prize for General Nonfiction. She is also the author of a young adult history of the civil rights movement, *A Dream of Freedom.* This essay was adapted from a speech she gave at the University of the South in the fall of 2002, which was reprinted in the *Sewanee Theological Review.*

PAULI MURRAY was the author of *Proud Shoes: The Story of an American Family* (1956). She was a labor activist, poet, attorney, and the first African American woman to be ordained a priest in the Episcopal Church. She died in 1985.

SENA JETER NASLUND is a native of Birmingham and winner of the Harper Lee Award. Naslund is the author of *Ice Skating at the North Pole, The Animal Way to Love, Sherlock in Love, The Disobedience of Water, Ahab's Wife,* and *Four Spirits.* She is Distinguished Teaching Professor at the University of Louisville; program director of the Spalding University brief-residency Master of Fine Arts in Writing; and 2003 Vacca Professor, along with her husband, physicist John C. Morrison, at the University of Montevallo, Alabama.

SYLVIA RHUE is the director of religious affairs and constituency development for the National Black Justice Coalition in Washington, D.C. A religious scholar, writer, and filmmaker, Rhue was the coalition manager for the California Freedom to Marry Coalition and the director of Equal Partners in Faith. She was a coproducer, with Dee Mosbacher and Frances Reid, of the award-winning film on homosexuality and the black church, *All God's Children.* Rhue earned a bachelor's degree from Oakwood College in Huntsville, Alabama, a master's degree in social work from UCLA, and a doctorate in human sexuality at the Institute for the Advanced Study of Human Sexuality, San Francisco.

JESSICA ROSKIN is a cantor at Temple Emanu-El in Birmingham. She is the current president of the Southside Faith Communities, a group of clergy and religious leaders in downtown Birmingham. She is also a member of the Interfaith Leadership Institute of The National Conference for Community and Justice. This is her first published piece of nonfiction.

MAB SEGREST joined the faculty of Connecticut College in fall 2002. She was acting department chair for the 2003–2004 academic year and was appointed Fuller-Maathai Professor of Gender and Women's Studies in July 2004. Segrest is a writer, teacher, and organizer. She has been active in antiracist, feminist, lesbian/gay, and economic justice movements for more than twenty years. Her first book, *My Mama's Dead Squirrel: Lesbian Essays on Southern Culture,* was published by Firebrand Books in 1985. Her second book, *Memoir of a Race Traitor,* narrates her work against Klan and neo-Nazi movements in the 1980s. Her third book, *Born to Belonging: Writings on Spirit and Justice,* was published by Rutgers University Press.

LEE SMITH is the author of three story collections and nine novels. Her stories and articles have appeared in many periodicals and anthologies including *Redbook,* the *New York Times,* and *Atlantic Monthly.* She is a professor in the English department at North Carolina State University and has received numerous awards and honors, including the Lila Wallace/Reader's Digest Award, the Robert Penn Prize for Fiction, the O. Henry Award, and a fellowship at the Duke University Center for Documentary Studies.

JEANIE THOMPSON has published three collections of poetry: *How To Enter the River, Witness* (which won the Benjamin Franklin Award of the Publishers' Marketing Association), and *White for Harvest: New and Selected Poems.* Her poems have appeared widely in such magazines as *Black Warrior Review, Crazyhorse, Louisville Review, New England Review, North American Review, River Styx,* and *Southern Review.* She has received individual artist fellowships from the Louisiana Council on the Arts and the Alabama State Council on the Arts, has held a Walter Daken Fellowship at the Sewanee Writers Conference, and in 2002 was named Alumni Artist of the Year by the University of Alabama College of Arts and Sciences. Thompson has directed the Alabama Writers' Forum since its inception in 1993, and is a faculty member of the Spalding University Brief Residency MFA Writing Program in Louisville, Kentucky. She lives in Montgomery, Alabama.

JAN WILLIS is a professor of religion and Walter A. Crowell Professor of Social Studies at Wesleyan University. She is the author of *The Diamond Light, Dreaming Me, Enlightened Beings, On Knowing Reality,* and *The Tattwartha Chapter of Asanga's Bodhisattvabhumi.* She has studied with Tibetan Buddhists in India, Nepal, Switzerland, and the United States for more than three decades, and has taught courses in Buddhism for twenty-five years. One of the earliest American scholar-practitioners of Tibetan Buddhism, Professor Willis has published numerous essays and articles on Buddhist meditation, hagiography, and women and Buddhism.

Library of Congress Cataloging-in-Publication Data

All out of faith : Southern women on spirituality / edited by Wendy Reed and Jennifer Horne.
    p.   cm.
    ISBN-13: 978-0-8173-1534-4 (alk. paper)
    ISBN-10: 0-8173-1534-9 (alk. paper)
    1. Southern women—Religious life. 2. Women authors—Religious life. 3. Women and reli-
gion. 4. Spirituality. I. Reed, Wendy, 1966– II. Horne, Jennifer.
    BL625.7.A45 2006
    200.82′0975—dc22
                                                                        2006003881